SHADOWS
IN THE
STREAM

SHADOWS
IN THE
STREAM

SEASONAL APPROACHES
TO GAME FISHING

IAN NEALE

SWAN·HILL
PRESS

First published in the UK in 2000
by Swan Hill Press, an imprint of Airlife Publishing Ltd

British Library Cataloguing-in-Publication Data
A catalogue record for this book
is available from the British Library

ISBN 1 85310 783 2

Adapted from material first published in *Trout and Salmon* and *Salmon, Trout & Sea-trout*
magazine

Typeset by Rowland Phototypesetting Ltd, Bury St Edmunds, Suffolk
Printed in Hong Kong

Swan Hill Press
an imprint of Airlife Publishing Ltd
101 Longden Road, Shrewsbury, SY3 9EB, England
E-mail: airlife@airlifebooks.com
Website: www.airlifebooks.com

Acknowledgements

Where would we be without good friends? This book is the result of so many good friends, who over the years have been kind and supportive to me in many different ways! Through the high times and the low times, I owe much to the encouragement and loyalty of these friends. Special thanks therefore go to: Karen Yorke who has faithfully typed the manuscript and my fishing articles for over fifteen years now. I couldn't have done it without you Karen! Thanks also go to: Roy Eaton for all his editorial skills and who initially put much energy into the early stages of the book; Fred Whoriskey of the Atlantic Salmon Federation for all his help and co-operation in supplying the scientific research information and data for the Ponoi chapter; Dave and Tessa Konrath who have also spent many hours on the word processor trying to sort out my future.

George and Wendy Haywood, who have had to put up with me for the last five years. Thanks for your kindness and for being there.

A special thanks to Bill Currie who has been a great friend and mentor over the years and has had a huge influence on my life. Bill, I really appreciate your help and your time on the foreword.

Another really great guy is Mike Leach. Thanks for being a good friend and for all your support over the years, our times together on the river bank are very special and packed with fun and laughter – memories of happy days.

Thanks also to Annie who has played a very special part in my life – several of the photographic contributions included in this book were taken by her.

Last but not least, thanks to my very good friend Peter Heddle, who started me off with a fishing rod and line – just a few years ago now! Thank you Peter.

Thanks also to Frontiers International for allowing me the opportunity to experience the Ponoi River Operation and to be able to write about my time on this wonderful and unique Atlantic salmon river.

Dedication

This book is dedicated to Bob Lambert: a passionate angler and fly-tyer. A true friend and greatly missed.

Foreword

This book is part of the log of a remarkable fisher. In the course of a long fishing life, I have met many keen and knowledgeable fishers, but few have even approached the quality of Ian Neale. I do not merely mean that as a young man his fishing was outstanding and he was selected to fish for England. Fishing is about many things – knowing your rivers and lochs, understanding the fish and handling tackle with skill. The outstanding fishers of our day have had at least one other attribute – passion. Ian's enthusiasm and dedication to fly-fishing is powerful and seriously infectious. I have been lucky in being able to fish with him in a wide variety of places for some twenty-five years, from my first meeting with him on Ardleigh in Essex, to his home fishings on Mull in the Inner Hebrides and to a great array of beats on rivers throughout Scotland. I got used to Ian wiping my eye. He was adept at picking out two-pounders on Mishnish apparently by magic; he had extraordinary luck in taking the biggest February salmon on record on the Helmsdale; he could merge with the stillness of the night and tempt Scottish sea trout superbly. It is not only the successes which recommend Ian; it is the determined, deeply enthusiastic concentration he brings to fishing. He invents highly successful flies and 'Neale variants' and he handles his rods with impressive skill. Above all, as this book shows in rich detail, he has a special understanding of fish. What does that really mean? I believe it is part of the often discussed phenomenon that the hunter loves his quarry. A passion for fishing goes hand in hand with a deep respect for fish and a caring approach to their environment. These qualities shine through Ian's fishing and writing. *Shadows in the Stream* is a memorable personal diary as well as a wider record of the delights of gamefishing.

BILL CURRIE

Contents

CHAPTER 1

FEBRUARY
BREAKING THE ICE

For some of us the salmon fishing close season is not too long. We can, if we are lucky, fish until the end of November on Nith and Tweed. Early January into February sees the opening of a new season, not least on the rivers of the far north and east coasts of Scotland – Halladale and Naver, Helmsdale and Thurso – all of which open on 11 January. The term 'spring fishing' applied to this early sport is a misnomer. It's more like midwinter fishing in most years. On early season trips to the Helmsdale, in north-east Sutherland, I have been known to take my cross-country skis, just in case conventional transport was snowed off! However, the reward of one of those glorious early salmon we call 'springers' makes any hardship worthwhile. On my first trip to the Helmsdale my own reward was a superb sea-liced fish of 28½lb – a heavy springer by any standard. Moreover, I caught it after I had already taken a splendid 10-pounder. That wasn't bad for a first spring outing; but such luck doesn't come every year, as the next season was to make plain. Whereas my first season had been mild and dry, with the gauge reading just one inch, the second brought heavy snow on the hills and below freezing temperatures at night, bringing the river to a

Falls – Pool below Kildonan Falls (in background). On the Helmsdale, lower Beat 6. The early salmon are usually held back in the lower beats below falls until water temperatures reach 42°F.

virtual standstill as thick ice packed tight against the banks. For me this was a new experience, and I remember walking the dog down to the water on my first morning to see the whole river moving slowly, and carrying a bank-to-bank raft of those floating ice crystals we call 'grue'.

Grue forms when the temperature of the water falls below freezing and particles of ice combine to form small globules in the water. These grow in size, joining with each other and forming a deep, floating mass of dense ice. Nothing can be done about it, for it completely covers the river and puts an end to fishing. Casting into it produces nothing more than a mass of ice crystals at the end of the line. All one can do is sit back and wait for a change in water temperature; as little as one degree can be enough to remove the menace, the water seeming to clear almost magically. This is the time to fish, for often, as the grue clears, the fish come suddenly on the take.

I remember one February day on the Aberdeenshire Dee when we sat in the hut waiting and watching for the grue to clear. It was a gloriously bright, sunny morning, with a hard ground frost only slowly giving way to the sun's warmth, but by 11 am the temperature had risen slightly and, sure enough, the grue crystals started to thin before our eyes. I walked down to the pool below and took a beautiful fresh fish of 9½lb on my second cast. Grue may be a curse and the source of much frustration, but its clearing can be a blessing.

On my second season on the Helmsdale I just couldn't believe my eyes as Bill Currie and I drove up river. Every pool was a mass of ice and grue. Were we really going to fish in this? Eventually we stopped off by Salscraggie Pool on Beat 1, where I had caught my first fish of the previous year. It brought a smile to my face; it was good to be back, despite the conditions.

Bill had fished the Helmsdale in February for many years and knew how to cope with such conditions – so too did our excellent gillie and friend Johnnie Sutherland, a lifelong Helmsdale man.

We inspected the pool carefully and to me the situation seemed impossible, with thick sheets of ice extending from each bank to leave a narrow channel of grue-covered water in the middle.

'What on earth do we do now, Bill?' I asked 'Well,' he said, 'you find the biggest piece of wood you can and we'll show you!'

By the time I had found a decent bit of wood, Bill and Johnnie were already in action, starting to break up the great sheets of ice at the bottom of the pool. I knew Bill to be slightly eccentric, but this was ludicrous! I joined them, however, and slowly we dismantled the thick wedges of ice at the bankside.

It was great fun breaking up the ice and pushing the rafts into the middle of the river. They would float slowly downstream and break into a million pieces as they hit the fast, shallow water below. The noise was incredible. By lunchtime we had cleared several pools and had warmed ourselves up considerably.

'Time for a gin and tonic,' said Bill.

'Wonderful idea,' I replied. 'G and T with a slice . . . but how about the ice?'

The ice was no problem, I walked down to the river's edge and broke some off some appropriately peat-stained pieces. Who could ask for more? Well, a salmon would be good, of course, but first things first!

We let the pool settle after lunch and fished down the faster, smaller pools below where icing hadn't been such a problem, though I did fish down the edge of one pool which was icy for 8–10ft. The wading was slightly precarious, but halfway down I pulled a fish. It was nothing spectacular, but enough for me to know that it was a fish. A change of fly was indicated and it was now that I was able to rest my rod flat on the table of ice beside me. 'Very handy,' I thought. It made changing the fly much easier.

Yes, I did hook the fish a few minutes later and, yes, I lost it. Such is life.

We fished on through the short winter afternoon and Bill had by now covered a fair distance, having fished down to the lowest pool before walking back up to where Johnnie and I were fishing, so he decided to fish Salscraggie for the last hour.

Having fished the headstream down to the middle, he noticed that a slight breeze was blowing upstream from the tail. Now Salscraggie is just one of many Helmsdale pools that are best fished by 'backing-up' (see diagram 1), a method used to fish slower, deeper pools where the flow is not sufficient to allow a fly to be fished in the conventional downstream manner. The pool is fished from the tail back upstream, the angler casting fairly square across the pool, taking three or four steps upstream and hand-lining the fly.

The technique is best used when an upstream breeze ripples the surface and breaks up the overall flatness of the water and the Helmsdale has many canal-like pools on which backing-up can be productive, especially on the lower beats. I remember fishing the Kilphedir Pool with Johnnie Sutherland one day, when about halfway down we saw a fish show towards the tail.

'That's a fresh fish, Ian,' said Johnnie. 'Quick! Let's get down and cover it!'

Baddie Wood Pool, lower Beat 4, Helmsdale. Often in early spring thick ice forms across every pool, making fishing conditions seem impossible. However, with determination and ice breaking procedures adhered to – pools can be cleared and made fishable!

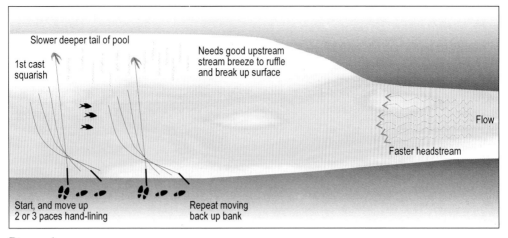

Diagram 1

We almost ran down to the lie and fished down over the fish, lying close to our bank. After I had fished down for ten yards or so, Johnnie said, 'Right, Ian. Now back it up'. Within three or four casts, and as I was slowly hand-lining back, I had a good, solid pull, and the fish was on. It was a lovely fresh springer of 7lb.

This incident certainly proved the worth of backing-up. It also demonstrated the worth of covering a fish which shows at this time of year – these springers are usually keen takers, and if a fish is in a lie, more often than not, it can be tempted to take the fly.

On this particular day on Salscraggie, Bill reckoned he had just enough breeze and, feeling a little more optimistic, backed-up the pool from the tail – but without so

Kilphedir Pool, Beat 2, Helmsdale River. The author is seen here 'backing-up' from the tail of the pool with the benefit of a good upstream breeze to break up water surface – a deadly method on these slower 'canal-like' stretches.

13

much as a pluck. Time was running out, and on what was to have been his last cast, his fly hit the roadside crash barrier on the back cast and cracked off.

Now most people, feeling tired after a hard day, with darkness coming in fast, and with the temperature falling, would at this stage have reeled in and called it a day – but not Bill. No, he went up to the road, found his fly, tied it back on in the gloaming, and went back down to the pool. Within minutes he was rewarded by a good, solid pull and was into a magnificent springer which, after a great fight, weighed 17lb. It would have been a beautiful fish at the best of times, but at the end of that cold February day it was superb.

Of course, February isn't always like that. It can be mild with the river running clear and free, with no sign of grue or bankside ice; but I shall still put my skis in the car before I make my way north next spring, and I shall go prepared for some ice-breaking if need be, in the knowledge that the potential reward, if it comes, will make it a day to remember for more reasons than one.

———————————

THE FISH OF A LIFETIME

How that second visit to the Helmsdale contrasted with my first, the year before. Then, never having fished for 'springers', I had been full of excitement and anticipation as I drove north on a late February day. I didn't know what to expect, as all my previous salmon fishing experience had been on small west coast rivers, where I had concentrated on grilse and summer salmon.

I joined Bill late on Tuesday afternoon, to find the river reading only one inch on the gauge. Sport was dour, and Bill and his guest, David, had taken only several well-mended kelts during the previous two days, with a fresh fish nowhere to be seen.

Next morning I was up bright and early and disappointed to find no change in the weather. Johnnie Sutherland expressed his concern about the lack of water and fish, however, he was confident that despite the conditions, one or two fish would be creeping into the river. His knowledge of the Helmsdale apart, he is a great companion and keeps you going all day. He marches down the bank like a drill-sergeant, and you have no chance of getting chilled even on the coldest of days!

As the water was so low, Johnnie suggested I fish a sink-tip with a 1½-in Waddington, Willie Gunn. Normally at this time of year one's line would be a medium-sinker, say a Wet-Cel 2, with a fly of 2–3in. The Rob Wilson Brora Waddington is particularly popular in this part of the world. It is tied on a heavy-gauge wire which takes the fly deeper. When the water is very cold, it is essential to get down to the fish and to put the fly across their noses. They do not normally move up to the fly as freely as in later spring and summer, when the water temperature is higher.

On this particular day the water temperature was an incredibly high 40°F, virtually unheard of in Sutherland in February. At the top of lower Beat 6, about halfway up the river, are the Kildonan Falls which normally hold the fish back until the temperature reaches 42°F, when they will take the falls without any problem. Fish had already been nosing the falls and several had ascended to the upper river; this was reflected in the fact that fewer fish were being caught in the lower river, which was a pity because today we were to fish Beat 1, the lowest beat on the river, adjoining the association water, close to the sea.

A stiff south-easterly wind blowing upstream made casting difficult and the morning was unproductive. I caught and returned just two kelts, which at least gave a little excitement.

After lunch Johnnie took me across to the far side of Salscraggie to fish down from the headstream. I had to cast really hard into the strong upstream wind, but with the stream running down hard on our side, a long line was not vital.

I had been fishing for only five minutes or so when the line was pulled hard and BANG! I was into my first spring salmon. It took well in the fast water, ran back across the river, showed its beautiful silver flank, turned, and then started running upstream with Johnnie and myself in hot pursuit. I was trembling with excitement when, after about ten minutes and with the fish on its side, Johnnie gently slipped it into the net. It was an incredible feeling. My first springer, a little more than 10lb and covered in sea-lice – an absolute corker!

Bill had been fishing the opposite bank, backing-up from the tail and he was equally jubilant as we walked back to the car to refresh ourselves with a well-earned dram.

Now I'm not a greedy fisherman and I was more than content with this one splendid fish. Indeed, I was anxious for my host to connect with a fish after two days without a touch.

Johnnie suggested that Bill should fish down from Salscraggie while we went to the lower river. February fishing days are short in Sutherland's far north and by the time we had fished from Upper Caen, the best of the day was gone. However, I waded carefully into the head of Lower Caen and started to fish down. Johnnie had pointed out a lie, and as I approached it, my fly swung round into the slack water and seemed to snag. I lifted the rod carefully, felt two decent pulls, then suddenly the reel screamed and my rod bent double.

Johnnie called me to get out of the river and up on to the bank as quickly as I could, and I remember that just as I tightened into the fish, another large fish showed slightly downstream. Johnnie had seen my fish and clearly it was not a kelt. I kept in touch with it as it started making its way back towards the North Sea and then, after a long run, it showed, throwing itself clear into the air. It looked big, and Johnnie thought that it was probably 16–18lb. I started to shake again!

Bill had seen Johnnie and I standing side by side as he fished down above us, but by the time he reached us, I had been playing the fish for nearly an hour, and still I couldn't make any impression on it. All I remember was that my right arm was nearly falling off. Poor old Bill couldn't believe it. He thought we had been passing the time talking together, then he was treated to the sight of the fish as it leapt for the umpteenth time. He and Johnnie agreed that it was a fine fish of 16–18lb.

It was now nearly dark and Johnnie suggested that Bill should finish off down at the Whinnie, which was as good a place as any in the fading light and with a run of fish plainly in the river. Just then Bill saw another fish show above us in Upper Caen – Things were looking better!

I played my fish for another twenty minutes and eventually had it on its side several hundred yards downstream from where I had hooked it. Johnnie went down the steep bank and into the water with my net, a good-sized salmon net and certainly capable of bagging a fish of 16–18lb.

Johnnie turned and looked up. 'Ian, the net's no' big enough! This salmon is all of 30lb.' 'Come on, Johnnie! This is no time for a joke!' I said. 'I'm no' kidding, Ian! It's a thirty-pounder!' Johnnie replied.

The net was unceremoniously thrown up the bank and Johnnie carefully edged into the water, then, even more carefully, he put one hand round the wrist of the fish's tail and another into its gill-cover. I'll never forget the sight of Johnnie pulling that huge salmon up the bank, its great back and belly bending in the middle with the strain.

'Look at this, Ian!' he said. 'It's a 30-pounder.'

He walked well up into the field before laying it carefully down and despatching it with my priest. Johnnie and I could hardly believe what we saw as we gazed at this magnificent cock salmon. Just a mile off the tide, it was covered in long-tailed sea-lice, with the fly well back in its mouth. Back at the hotel a little later it weighed a little more than 28½lb. It seemed incredible that a fish of that size could have made its way up in such low water.

It was, I believe, the biggest salmon off the Helmsdale for more than a decade, and the biggest February fish ever taken from the river. Walking shakily back to the car in the darkness, I reflected on my first day's spring salmon fishing; two fish for 38½lb! What an introduction! To catch a salmon of 28½lb is at any time the achievement of a lifetime, but to catch one on a fine spring day in February . . . What more can I say?

Fish of a lifetime – the author's second spring salmon. After taking a 10lb fish from Salscraggie he caught this superb sea-liced 28½lb fish from Lower Caen, Helmsdale, on a sink-tip line and 1½-in Willie Gunn Waddington.

CHAPTER 2

MARCH
A QUESTION OF CONFIDENCE

The day came when I was fortunate enough to be invited to fish for two days in spring on a middle beat of the Aberdeenshire Dee. A good friend, Rex, was taking his son back south (gallant chap that he is) and he insisted that I fish his rod for his last two days. As I was only just over the hill, on Speyside, how could I possibly refuse?

The fishing had been difficult, with only three fish taken so far for the week, and I had driven over the Lecht from Grantown to see the river at Ballater in full flood. An overnight deluge in the Cairngorms had brought the river up to 4ft.

The next morning brought a real feeling of spring and the river was falling away at 2ft 10in. It was slightly peaty, but clear enough for the fly. I hadn't taken my spinning rods anyway, so fly it was jolly well going to be, despite the fact that the opposition were hurling out all manner of ironmongery. The water temperature was 38°F which for February was incredible.

The Aros tube-fly – originally designed for fishing the Aros River on the Island of Mull, where the author owned his own fishing lodge. Easy to tie and based on a tadpole-style of dressing, it can be tied on brass, aluminium or plastic tubes. Dressing as follows:
Black-and-orange pattern –
Two lengths of black-and-orange bucktail or squirrel, tied side by side for wing and not overdressed. The body is either gold or silver lurex.
The author ties them in various colours but generally prefers the black-and-orange or black-and-yellow versions.

I had been warned by others in the party to follow the gillie's every instruction; otherwise I would soon be in his black book: 'If he says, "Try a Willie Gunn, Sir." you jolly well try a Willie Gunn. All right?'

After breakfast I made my way down to the pool with Rex, who was to spend an hour or so with me before heading south. He knew the beat well and was going to show me the lies until such time as Jimmy, our gillie, appeared. The pool looked magnificent and, despite the water running on the high side, I felt confident about fishing the fly. It was sunny and warm, so I opted for my favourite 1-in brass tube with a long Tadpole-style black-and-yellow hairwing dressing. I call it the Aros tube and I have caught many salmon on it and its black-and-orange sister.

I started in at the head stream and had fished for about half an hour before Jimmy arrived, having seen to other members of the party upstream. I walked up the bank to greet him and saw his eyes immediately fixed on my fly.

'Will this be all right?' I tactfully enquired, dreading a negative reply.

'Oh, aye sir! That will be fine for this water.' I breathed a great sigh of relief. I had passed the test – so far!

I fished on carefully over the next hour and felt that my Wet-Cel 2 line and small tube-fly were fishing at just the right depth. Certainly two well-mended kelts took a liking to the fly, adding to my own confidence. Rex left at about 11 am and I carried on down the delightful stretch of water.

Then Jimmy returned and, despite my confident rumblings, uttered the dreaded words:

'Try a Willie Gunn, Sir.'

I came off the water for him to rummage through my boxes of flies, his eyes fixed on the biggest Brora Waddington in the collection.

'Oh, no,' I thought as he pulled the creature from the bottom of the box.

'Aye. Try that, Sir.'

My confidence dropped by 80% as I endeavoured to launch this missile into the middle of the Dee, but I fished on for several minutes or so until he decided to resume his rounds. Now, a gillie, and in particular a gillie who has been on the water for thirty years, has to be respected for his advice. He knows every inch, rock and stone on the beat so I would never go against his professional opinion – normally, that is.

Today, however, the second he disappeared, I was out of the water and had quickly changed back to my 1-in tube, the black-and-orange version this time. Within two minutes I had hooked another well-mended kelt which fought like a fresh fish for all its worth.

'That's more like it!' I said to myself. My confidence had risen back to 99% and I felt happy.

Jimmy returned just before lunch and, seeing him coming, I quickly reeled in and walked back towards the hut frantically trying to conceal my favourite fly. In a slight panic, I managed to get all three treble hooks embedded in my woolly jumper sleeve. Annie came to my rescue and soon extracted the hooks and somehow or other we managed to keep the fly out of Jimmy's sight, for I did not wish to end up in his little black book – not on day one, anyway!

After lunch I was taken up to the top beat and, to my relief, Jimmy said he would follow on in a while. On the far bank the opposition came out of his hut and armed with a rather large Blair spoon, started to bombard the pool – snagging on nearly every cast, I might add.

The reward of confidence – a beautiful fresh spring salmon of 9lb plus taken on a black-and-orange Aros tube (brass version) lies on the ground amongst the snowdrops in early March.

'That's all right,' I thought, 'he'll most probably drive the fish over to my side.' Anyway, I always love to follow the opposition down and try to take a fish out from behind him – especially when he's spinning!

My confidence was still on a high, and as long as I could carry on with that fly and get away with it, I would be happy.

I started in below the big rock, fishing off the bank as Jimmy had instructed. On the fourth cast the fly swung gently round in the stream, I felt a slight knock, then a long, hard pull, and I just let the fish take line as the reel screamed. What a magical moment – what a magical sound!

I lifted the rod and tightened; downstream I could see Jimmy talking to another rod. They both looked up as my reel screamed and so did the chap opposite, the fish fought hard and stayed deep with the occasional head-shaking. This one was no kelt.

Jimmy walked up towards me and picked up my net, a brief discussion followed by a sighting of the fish confirmed that it was indeed a fresh springer. My legs shook!

Seven or eight minutes later the salmon was on its side, a beautiful bar of silver and Jimmy slipped the net under my first fresh fish of the season – 9lb plus. I was delighted.

I saw that all three hooks were well engaged in the scissors. Now was the time of reckoning! Jimmy bent down to extract the hooks.

'I hope you don't mind, Jimmy, but I thought I'd try a change of fly, back to an old favourite tube.' 'Oh, no! That's fine, Sir, that's fine. Well done!'

He picked up the fish, shook me by the hand and told me to carry on down the pool and into the next, which I obligingly did. I felt I was on a roll now and if any other fish were in the pool, I would catch them. It wasn't to be, however, but I was more than content with my one beautiful springer.

Next day I was taken down to the middle beat, and Jimmy said he would walk down the two pools with me, pointing out the various hot-spots as we went. 'What flies do you think, Jimmy?' I asked. 'Oh, that wee tube you had on yesterday. That'll be just right for here, Sir!'

I had been reprieved and given the ultimate blessing by my gillie. For once my confidence reached 100%.

By mid-April the upper and middle reaches of the River Spey are yielding crops of fine spring salmon to keen anglers and just the mention of Pitchroy, Ballindalloch, Tulchan and Castle Grant sets the adrenalin flowing. However, on this occasion I was heading for a slightly less well-known upper beat at Kincardine, situated near Boat of Garten. The Kincardine beat is approximately two miles long with fourteen named pools and streams. Kincardine is shared with the opposite bank Kinchurdy, which is owned by the Strathspey Estate in Grantown-on-Spey. Both beats have a carefully planned sharing arrangement which ensures tenants on both sides are able to fish both banks without the worry of opposition rods. The beats are simply divided into upper and lower and are rotated every lunchtime. The two estates have also agreed to operate a well managed improvement plan, the Oyster Catcher pool has already been deepened at the headstream and this pool has shown a significantly higher catch-rate performance, as we were just about to find out!

Michael and I had arrived to find fresh snowfall on the surrounding hills and as we drove towards the beat the snow continued to fall. It is always unpredictable at this time of year, weather and water conditions change quickly with fluctuating air and water temperatures. Sometimes you will fish with sinking lines and large flies or sinktips and on occasions it will be a floating line and smaller flies, but conditions are unpredictable so go well prepared.

Spinning is always popular in the spring and Michael has developed his spinning technique into a fine art. He only fishes the one pattern which he calls his 'Wee Red Devon', however, his Red Devon comes in three different sizes 2in, 1½in and 1in, which he uses, depending on water conditions, temperature, rate of flow, etc. These 'Wee Red Devons' have a central copper tube built on a fibreglass shell. He very rarely uses the 2-in version, and even on such a large river as the Spey he has achieved most success with the 1½-in and the 1-in. No other weight is attached or needed and the Devon is fished off the line with a swivel attached some 18-in above the bait. As with fly-fishing the ingredients of success are down to proper presentation. The Devon is cast squarely into midstream and allowed to drift round in the current, in other words, there is no need to touch the reel handle at all. Mike keeps his rod tip high to allow the 'Wee Devon' to sink and drift, and he keeps his index fingertip on the nylon by the reel at all times in order to keep in touch with any movement, etc. Another advantage of the 'Wee Devon' is that by its very nature and size it causes hardly any disturbance when cast into the water, just a tiny plop and it is working! In all the time I have watched Michael working this Devon I have only known him to lose one of these spinning baits, but that is another story!

We arrived at the hut by 9 am to be met by our gillie, Norman Stone. The water height was showing just over one foot on the gauge and the temperature was 42°F. Norman was very enthusiastic and optimistic and told us that good numbers of fish had been coming through the beat all week. The two rods fishing the day before had taken two sea-liced fish of 13 and 8lb respectively – We couldn't get tackled-up fast enough!

I decided to fish the fly with my 15½-ft Diawa amorphous rod, sinktip line and a 1½-in black-and-orange Waddington. Norman was keen for us to fish the Oyster Catcher pool and suggested that Michael fished off the near bank towards the slower and deeper tail of the pool with his 'Wee Devon'. Norman was going to row me across to fish from the other bank down through the faster headstream, following Michael down. As we rowed across and looked down, Norman and I both noticed that Michael appeared to be into a fish already – I couldn't believe it, I hadn't even wetted my line yet. 'Bloody typical of him,' I said, 'Can't take him anywhere, Norman!'

By now the weather had improved, the sun was shining and it felt more like spring once again. Michael had taken his fish within half a dozen casts on the 1½-in 'Wee Red Devon'. I managed to take several pictures as Michael played and netted his fish, a beautiful bright and solid 11½-lb cock fish. Michael was delighted, you could now begin to feel the air temperature begin to rise as the day warmed and brightened.

I fished down through the pool, but had a feeling that maybe I wasn't fishing quite deep enough in the cold and clear snow-melt water. Michael went back up to the headstream and followed me down on the far bank and it wasn't long before he was into number two. Yet again, a solid fish of just over 9lb and showing several sea-lice, bearing in mind that this beat is over 60 miles from the sea. Clearly these spring fish were running fast and hard. There were more pictures and more congratulations as Michael's fish was slipped carefully into his Gye net.

After lunch we changed over and went down onto the lower beat. Norman took me over into the far bank and I walked up to fish a pool called the Groyne, a really super, streamy little pool which involves a short wade from the bank; but one has to be careful not to go too far or one will be standing on top of one's fish!

Michael by now had abandoned his spinning rod for the fly. He was fishing his 15-ft Bruce and Walker Expert and had opted for a Wet-Cel 2 sinking line with a 1½-in firefly Waddington. He fished from the Bay Window down and followed me through the Groyne. I was

What to fish, fly or spinner? The 1-in Wee Red Devon is smaller than the Waddington fly and was responsible for the capture of this fine spring salmon.

nearly through the pool and beginning to reel in and Michael was about halfway down, when I heard a commotion and turned my head to see a big fish falling back into the water. Mike lifted his rod, but the hooks fell out, and he shook his head in disbelief, muttering that it was a fish in excess of 15lb. From what I had seen it would appear to have been an extremely large fish – he was certainly having some wonderful sport! As the afternoon wore on, weather conditions began to deteriorate as a nasty upstream squally wind developed with occasional heavy snow showers. The river went dead and we saw no more signs of fish as we fished on in the fading light. For Michael it had been a most exciting and rewarding day's spring fishing. I recall Norman's parting comment to us: 'Not bad for a beat that isn't even on the map!' I couldn't have agreed more!

Mike Leach looks clearly happy with these two springers taken on his 1 ½-in Wee Red Devon from the Kincardine beat, River Spey.

CHAPTER 3

APRIL
NEW ZEALAND INTERLUDE

I always love to fish new waters and to learn of new fishing techniques and fly patterns, and to make new friends in the process. So, when the chance came to visit New Zealand, it was something not to be missed, despite the fact that it would be at the back-end of their season and would take me away from Scotland's rivers at a prime time in our spring.

Only a day after arriving in Wellington and still feeling jet-lagged, I was invited to fish the famous Tongariro river for the weekend with two friends of the aunt with whom I was staying. Almost before I realised what was happening, we were driving north after a 7 am start. We would, I was assured, be fishing by midday.

My companions were Gillian van Raalte and Ian Routley, both fly-fishing fanatics, and by the time we arrived at Turangi in mid-morning, they really had my adrenalin flowing with their stories of previous days on the river. It had been helped, too, by that ubiquitous habit of fishermen of stopping to peer over bridges as each river is crossed and by Turangi's own special roadside welcome: 'Welcome to Turangi, fishing capital of the world'.

Ian and Gillian are members of the Tongariro and Lake Taupo Angling Club, which has an impressive clubhouse at Turangi. It consists of a fine sitting-room, with a long fire and fly-tying bench, a kitchen with freezers, cookers and microwaves and a well equipped gutting room and smokehouse. After fishing you can come back to the lodge, clean your fish, and put them into the smokehouse to be ready for you to take home. Ten twin-bedded cabins complete the complex. As we unloaded the car, a fellow member walked into the clubhouse with a rainbow trout which weighed in at 10½lb. It was my first sight of one of these legendary trout and it left a lasting impression. It had been caught in the Judge's Pool on a Red Rabbit lure.

The Tongariro, flowing into Lake Taupo, is a big, wide river running crystal-clear with long, deep holding pools and cascading rapids between them. It reminded me in many ways of some of our larger Scottish east-coast salmon rivers, such as Dee or Tweed. Taupo is virtually an inland sea, with rich feeding, such as crayfish and koura for its wild rainbow trout. These trout feed in the lake for most of the year and then, driven by their spawning instincts, enter the feeder rivers for their upstream spawning redds. The Tongariro is the largest of these feeders, although many smaller streams also offer excellent sport.

Several days' rain had brought all the rivers into spate when we arrived and the water was quite coloured. Local advice was that we should make for the headwaters and leave the main river for the next day.

Ten miles upstream we found a delightful stretch of water to fish. I had a wonderful feeling just being on this magnificent river and the surroundings were breathtaking. It was twelve noon, my hosts had been as good as their word.

The day turned hot beneath a clear blue sky and I found it hard to believe that this was the start of winter! We agreed to go our separate ways and meet up about three hours later, alas, when we did so it was to find that we had all drawn blank, it was time to try further downstream and to hope that the river had cleared a little.

Ian and Gilly opted to fish the Blue Pool – a long, deep, slow-moving pool with a fast headstream and the best lies, under the far bank, demanding deep wading and long casting.

Two main types of fishing are followed on the Tongariro: downstream wet-fly and upstream nymphing. I was to discover upstream nymphing later on, but we started with conventional downstream wet.

Single-handed rods of 9–10ft are ideal and with the fish tending to lie deep at this time of year, most people choose to fish with a high-density sinking line, usually a shooting-head. It is important to get your fly right down and with the low water temperature, it is wise to watch your step when wading. Favourite fly patterns for downstream wet are lure types, which include Red Setter, Red Rabbit, Hamill's Killer, Fuzzy Wuzzy, Muddler variations and Marabou lures, but only single hooks are allowed. The best sizes seem to be 6s and 8s, depending on the height and colour of the water.

We had about an hour's daylight left when we arrived at the Blue Pool and the water was still quite coloured. Ian put me to fish the fast, streamy headwater and slowly work my way down. Gilly followed and Ian brought up the rear.

It was Ian who was first to score as suddenly I heard a fish jump above me and Ian's reel screamed and his rod bent double. Gilly and I both got out of the water to watch the battle and a good, hard fight it was, until after ten to twelve minutes Ian beached a beautiful fresh-run rainbow of a little less than 4lb. Short and deep, with a small

Ian Routley caught the first fish – a fine, fresh-run rainbow trout of just under 4lb from the Blue Pool – using a 'Granny's Fur Coat' fly. I didn't feel I should go too deeply into its origin!

down a pool, he would always ask if he could fish at the tail of the pool only, or would follow us down from the head, casting upstream, this may sound odd, but it did work. Sometimes we came to a pool full of nymphers moving neither up nor down, so we would move on and find another pool.

On this occasion it was Bob who asked if he might fish the pool, so, being in need of a rest, I decided to sit on the bank and watch him at work. He had been on the water for only a few minutes when he struck into a fresh fish of just over 3½lb, it roared across the pool and up and down and really gave Bob a run for his money. He hooked and lost another three fish in the next half-hour, while the wet-fly fishers had not so much as a pluck! When Bob came out of the water I asked him if he could show me how to fish this intriguing method.

We prepared my rod with a size 7 floating line and a cast of about 15ft. Onto this he tied not one but two heavily leaded size 10 nymphs – but it was the manner in which he did this which I found intriguing. First, he tied on a nymph in the usual way, but then he tied a 12-in length of nylon to the *bend* of the hook and attached the second nymph, the point fly, to the end of that nylon (see diagram 2). He had one more vital piece to add to complete the set-up: a small piece of yellow or orange polystyrene which is slipped onto the top of the cast, tight against the join to the fly-line, to act as a strike-indicator. This floats on the surface and bobs or dips beneath the surface for a fraction of a second whenever a fish goes for one of the nymphs. Without it this method of fishing would be virtually impossible on the Tongariro; the

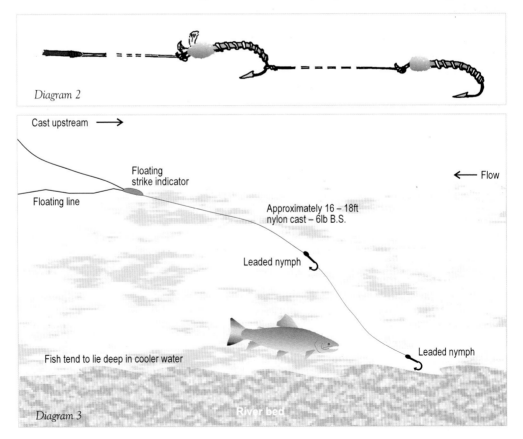

Diagram 2

Cast upstream ⟶

Floating
strike indicator

⟵ Flow

Floating line

Approximately 16 – 18ft
nylon cast – 6lb B.S.

Leaded nymph

Fish tend to lie deep in cooler water

Leaded nymph

Diagram 3

River bed

river runs so fast that feeling a take would be impossible. The trout mouth the nymphs quickly and gently, and an immediate strike is needed at the slightest indication. Depending on the speed of your reaction, you either find yourself solidly hooked into New Zealand or witness a fantastic 'explosion' as a silver fish leaps from the water before running like mad for Lake Taupo.

Fishing with a 15-ft cast and two heavily leaded nymphs and a strike-indicator can make for some interesting casting, but Bob waded beside me to offer words of advice as I moved through the pool. The upstream nymph demands reasonably long casting and a fairly fast retrieve with continuous mending of the line as the flies drift back towards you. Achieving a good 'drift' is the key to success, but with so much to think about, I wondered whether I would ever master the technique. However, after several practice casts, and plenty of advice in my left ear, I started to make sense of it. We fished right through the pool, but, alas, the fish had gone off the take. Deciding to rest the water for an hour or so, we retreated to a shady spot on the bank to sit down and sink another cold beer.

Further tuition was to come from John Morton, a professional fly-tyer from Christchurch and a friend of Bob, whom we met on the bank. Walking slowly back upstream with me, John stopped at small pockets of water off the main pools to show me all the likely lies. It was fascinating to be with him and to watch and learn from his skilful know-how, and to have my own casting technique polished up. Alas, despite his efforts and patience, we both remained fishless.

I had never come across such an unusual method of attaching droppers before, and I must admit that I was rather sceptical about its hooking qualities. However, I followed Bob and John's instructions to the letter and found over the next few days just how effective and simple the method is. I later showed it to a friend, Peter Heddle, when he came to visit me in Scotland. Like me, he was intrigued and decided to try it on one of our lochs. He returned in the evening with a lovely grilse of 5½lb.

If others are sceptical about the method, I can only say that I fished it during the rest of my stay in New Zealand and found it 100% satisfactory. I lost not one fish on it. It obviously has limitations for fishing in this country and is certainly of no use to loch-style drifters. Nymph fishermen, however, will find it certainly worth a try.

The most popular patterns on the Tongariro seemed to be Bug-eyed Nymphs of various designs, the Hare-and-copper (similar to our Hare's-ear Nymph), Pheasant Tail, Peacock Nymph and a caddis-type nymph. They are normally heavily dressed with as much as 12ins of lead wire down the bodies. Using two nymphs means that one can go deeper and have a greater chance of a fish.

It was before the crack of dawn next morning that Gilly was again rattling on our doors, stirring us up for another enormous breakfast. Stones Pool was the first objective and it was to prove the biggest I had fished so far. The sky was lightening as we tackled-up and waded halfway across to start to fish down towards the tail. Two other anglers were 100yd ahead of us and the going was so slow that it was light by the time we were well down the pool – and without so much as a pluck. I watched the two other anglers reach the tail and saw them each take a good fresh fish of 3½–4lb. I thought my turn must come at any minute as I approached the tail, but instead an eruption came from upstream as an angler following us down hooked into something enormous. We watched with mouths agape as he tackled the huge fish until at last he was able to beach a beautiful brown trout of 11–12lb. I had never

A beautiful brown trout of between 11–12lb taken on a Red Setter from Stones Pool. Note the depth of the fish and abundant spots – a true specimen.

before seen a trout like it; neither had its captor – it had taken the popular Red Setter.

It was becoming another beautiful, bright New Zealand day, with plenty of warmth in the air, but after several hours' hard work we were still fishless. Mark you, the scenery was some consolation, with Mount Ruapehu showing a heavy covering of fresh snow.

Deciding to go our separate ways, I headed back to the Birches, intent on developing my new-found nymphing technique. Ian and Gilly set off to try further up at the Blue Pool again. They aren't really interested in upstream nymphing and prefer to fish the conventional downstream wet-fly. We agreed to meet for lunch at 12.30.

The Birches was occupied so I decided to walk upstream to quieter waters to explore some of those little pockets again. They were hardly ever fished, mainly because they weren't recognised as main holding pools; but as I found out, they are often deep and just the place for running fish to stop for a rest, and ideal for the upstream technique. I decided to try a Hare-and-copper and a Bug-eye; with the swallows dipping over the water, the signs looked good.

I waded carefully in at the tail by a fallen tree, and my first cast was perfect, my two nymphs plopped in well, upstream. I made a couple of quick mends to the line, and the drift looked good. The little yellow indicator floated back towards me . . . Then, as it passed a submerged rock, it dipped, just for a second, and I struck fast . . . BANG! The water seemed to explode as a huge rainbow leapt several feet into the air and took off downstream like a torpedo.

Hastily gaining the bank, I managed to turn the fish back into the pool. It was a darkish jack fish of 3½–4lb and I held on and played it well as I looked for a likely place to beach it . . . then it turned over, the hook pulled out, and it was gone – my knees were knocking; my legs felt like jelly.

At least I had mastered the upstream nymph technique, and my confidence had a boost, I decided to rest the water – and myself – for a few minutes!

Several casts later, and on another good drift, my indicator again bobbed under. I struck hard and another fish leapt into the sky – only this time it was much bigger and absolutely silver fresh. What an incredible sight! The reel screamed as the fish raced away downstream, I couldn't believe its power. I was onto my backing before I could reach the bank, and still the fish was running.

By now the fish was into the rapids and had the upper hand, tight in under the far bank. All I could do was follow and try to recover line, but trying to follow a fish, while scrambling through the undergrowth on the banks of the Tongariro is not easy, especially in chest waders. I must have presented an amusing sight for any non-fisher passing by! I must have steeple-chased for 200yd before I was finally back into Upper Birches, which, luckily, nobody else was fishing.

I was now able to retrieve line fast, but the fish still had plenty of steam and was trying to take me out of this pool too! However, with most of my line back on the reel, I could keep control and see the fish in the clear water. Positioning myself on a small sandy beach, after a few more minutes I was able to get the fish on its side and bring it gently ashore.

It was a superb-looking fish, short, deep, with a very small head, an absolute bar of silver straight up from Lake Taupo and weighing a little more than 5lb. Again I was shaking with excitement as I pulled the Hare-and-copper from its jaw – I had cracked it!

Back upstream, I waded back into my little pool, by now well rested. A few casts later my indicator dipped again, I struck, and was doing battle with another fresh fish, which I was able to hold in the pool. This one was barely 3lb, but again a lovely silver fish. It had taken the bug-eyed variation of the Hare-and-copper. It was, I thought, time for lunch.

Back at the car-park I found that Gilly had also taken a lovely fresh fish of 3lb off the Blue Pool and on her old favourite the Red Setter. My 'hot-spot' soon called, and back by the fallen tree I started to work my way slowly upstream again. Straight away my indicator settled into a good drift, bobbed under, and another hard-fighting rainbow was on, again on the Bug-eyed Nymph. This fresh 4-pounder was soon followed by one of 3½lb; I couldn't believe this sport. The little pool was plainly full of fish, and all in taking mood.

A rest was indicated, and with a can of cool beer I was at peace with the world as I sat and watched the swallows flying fast and low over the water, picking off hatching flies. It was a glorious day, and very warm, a pair of bell-birds were busy in the bushes behind, uttering their exotic calls over an incredible vocal range. Across the river a pair of whistling blue ducks worked slowly upstream. Yes, life was good.

The fish still called, and back in the water I hadn't long to wait before the strike indicator twitched to signal the take of fish number five, 4½lb, also on the Bug-eye. Further up the pool, close to the headstream, trying to keep an eye on the indicator was much harder. I missed several good takes and hit the bottom at least a dozen times, which didn't do my hooks any good at all. Then, as the nymphs bounced along the bottom, I saw a little twitch and struck. All hell was let loose as a magnificent fish took to the air. He went crazy, shooting up and down the pool and taking to the air at least half a dozen times. It was heart-stopping stuff! I did manage to hold him in the pool despite his several attempts to reach the rapids, and ten minutes later I had him on his side at my feet. He was the best fish so far, fresh, weighing 5lb 10oz and on the Hare-and-copper on the point. It was a fitting climax to a wonderful day, for time had slipped by and at nearly four o'clock I had to join Ian and Gilly for our return to Wellington.

I was indeed content as I walked back to meet them, reflecting on the day's events; six fantastic wild rainbow trout taken from a river I had only dreamed about until two days before, and all taken on the upstream nymph. It was, without doubt, the most exciting fishing I had ever encountered.

The author looks delighted with this bag of wild Tongariro rainbow trout up to 5lb 10oz and all taken from a quiet stretch of water on upstream nymph and strike indicator method.

CHAPTER 4

MAY
DISCOVERING THE A'AN

I love to explore the tributaries of major salmon rivers. On their day they can be as productive as the main river and some of them can be considered as rivers in their own right. One is the Avon (pronounced A'an), the principal tributary of the Spey, entering the main river at Ballindalloch and my first chance to fish it came while I was hosting a fishing course at Seafield Lodge at Grantown and was offered three days on the Ballindalloch Castle water in early June.

The Avon is an important spawning tributary of the Spey and certainly the longest, its system covering some 50 miles. Its source is Loch Avon, many miles south at the foot of Beinne Mheadhain in the Cairngorms and indeed only a short distance from Pools of Dee, the source of the Aberdeenshire Dee.

My companion on the Avon was to be Peter Miller, who was bubbling with excitement when I arrived because rain had been falling hard and our chances looked promising. Despite my eight-hour drive, I couldn't wait: 'Come on, Peter, let's go and have a look now!'

Butler's Pool – Ballindalloch, River Avon. The major tributary of the River Spey, some 50 miles in length, its source is Loch Avon high in the Cairngorms and only a short distance from Pools of Dee. The River Avon can run incredibly clear as shown in the photo.

The Avon flows down a delightful and spectacular valley, with high green hills towering above. The smattering of whisky distilleries along the way had a different sort of attraction!

We soon found the gillie, Ian Galland, a young Englishman who had sold up in the south and moved north to be employed as resident gillie at Ballindalloch – lucky chap! Having fished the river for many years, he knew every nook and crannie where a fish might be taken.

'Two salmon and three sea-trout so far today,' he said.

Sure enough, five gleaming fish lay in the back of his Land Rover. What a sight to greet me after such a long journey – my excitement grew!

'We've a lot of fish in the river, and an especially good head of sea-trout,' Ian said. 'The river's high and peaty, but provided we don't get any more rain, it should be perfect for your three days.'

Good luck indeed!

Peter and I were up early next morning, having been instructed to fish Beat 2 in the morning and to go on to Beat 3 after lunch. Ian was there to greet us, the river had fallen off by several inches and was starting to clear, and the weather, too, had changed, with sunshine from a clear blue sky. It was warm as we walked up to the top of the beat.

We fished carefully down each pool until lunchtime, but without an offer, and I couldn't help feeling that the water was still rather high. After lunch on Beat 3, the afternoon became very warm, and the only response to our efforts was a tentative pluck

Upper Craigroy, River Avon, Ballindalloch. The gillie had consistently emphasised the point 'Always let your fly swing into the side and dangle on this river'. This advice was to prove invaluable to the author.

from a fish in the tail of Polldubh, which I thought was almost certainly from a sea-trout. We fished in the fading light of evening, and then, at about ten o'clock Peter hooked and landed a beautiful fresh-run sea-trout of 3½lb on a small tube-fly, it was good to see a fish on the bank. However, despite seeing several other fish during the next half-hour, we just couldn't arouse their interest, my feeling was that a run of sea-trout had come into the pool and moved quickly up river.

Next morning the river had dropped a further 6 inches and had cleared considerably. We were on Beat four in the morning, enticing, ideal fly water. I was fishing my 14-ft Bruce and Walker Hexagraph (Walker), which is a joy to fish on a river such as the Avon, but with the water clearing I took off my intermediate DT 11 line and put on a floater and size 10 Ally's Shrimp – my favourite!

Ian Galland had consistently emphasised one point: 'Always let your fly swing in to the side and dangle on this river. Let the fish come to the fly is what we say here.' I had always assumed that I did let the fly fish into the side and dangle, but it now seemed that I hadn't been letting it dangle for long enough! We must all be guilty of this from time to time, thinking, 'That's it,' and eager to cast across the pool again.

Ian's advice was to prove invaluable after I had reached Factor's and he had joined me again. It was bright and sunny and I entrusted him with my camera to take a few shots as I fished down. He pointed out various hot-spots, and kept on reminding me to fish the fly right in to the side, if I lifted a moment too soon, he would metaphorically rap me over the knuckles!

The Factors Pool, River Avon, Ballindalloch. Fishing a floating line and size 10 Ally's Shrimp fly, the author hooked and landed this fresh-run 6½-lb salmon.

Near to the end of the streamy water the fly seemed to be taking an age to work its full course and I was only half concentrating, engaged in conversation with Ian, a ploy to be recommended! I was actually looking at him with the fly literally dangling way below me, when the line tightened, the reel screamed and Ian calmly said 'That's him!'

I couldn't believe it. The fly had been hanging in flat water, yet this fish had apparently followed and followed and waited and waited before – BANG! – he really did take hold. It was the most exciting take, the fish took off and tore all over the pool, but six or seven minutes later it was on its side and I slipped it carefully over Ian's waiting net. It was a beautiful fresh-run 'bar of silver' weighing just 6½lb, with both hooks truly embedded in its upper jaw! The afternoon became very dour with bright hot conditions and by early evening we had both decided on an early bath and a large celebratory dram. After all it was my first salmon off the Avon!

The weather had changed once again by the following morning, and it had become cooler with more than a hint of rain in the air. Peter had work to do in the hotel, so I was to fish Beat six on my own. A pool called Butler's dominates this beat and easy wading on a light gravel bed made it enjoyable fishing. Staying with the floating line and my faithful Ally's, I started to work my way down, the river was in superb ply, and the sight of a hefty salmon rolling halfway down under the far bank really made the adrenaline flow. However, that fish seemed not to notice my efforts.

'Down at the tail, opposite those three oak trees,' said a voice from behind. 'That's where you'll get him.'

It was Ian, on cue as it were. I carefully fished on down, with my attentive gillie chatting to me once again. Could it happen a second time? Yes, it could and did – just where he had said. With my eyes on Ian, in full flow once again, and my line dangling immediately downstream I suddenly felt a fantastic pull and the reel screamed even harder – what a wonderful sensation that is!

The fish leapt clear once, twice, three times, still taking line. 'That's a good sea-trout,' said Ian.

Sure enough, several hectic minutes of sheer enjoyment later I was able to beach a magnificent sea-trout of over 4lb and as fresh as fresh could be.

'Did you see where your fly was when he took, Ian?'

'Yes,' I replied.

'There you are, you see: let the fish come to the fly, that's what we say here!'

Well, that little lesson had twice proved correct. Who was I to argue?

PURPLE HAYS – A SALMON AND SEA-TROUT FLY FOR SPRING AND SUMMER ON THE SPEY

After a hectic few weeks running fishing courses on Speyside (A'an) it's always good to be able to spend a few days fishing by myself before returning south.

Last May I stayed with my friends George and Wendy Haywood at Grantown-on-Spey and went straight to Mortimer's Tackle Shop to buy myself a weekly ticket to fish on the Grantown-on-Spey Association Water. It really is a first class stretch of water, commanding over seven miles of double bank fishing together with the River Dulnain which is one of the main tributaries of the River Spey.

May is a wonderful month to be in Strathspey, with the chance of a beautiful fresh spring salmon and of course the first big run of sea-trout, it can be a fisherman's dream come true. However, the first few days were very hard going as the water level had fallen and a strong easterly wind had developed blowing hard upstream making casting quite awkward. The weather pattern began to change and a mixture of rain, sleet and snow began to materialise. I had already heard of good numbers of fish downstream and felt sure that even a small lift in water height would change our luck, little did I know what was in store!

By the end of the week with the onset of heavier persistent rain and sleet the mighty Spey began to show slight signs of movement as the burns and tributaries began to fill. However, it was not long before the rain and sleet began to change to a heavy fall of snow and as the cold east wind eased during the morning, so the snow fell heavier and heavier and soon began to settle. I looked all around me to see the white hills and wondered if this could really be 15 May. As the day progressed and the weather turned more severe the river became deserted of anglers except, that is, for George and myself! We had been on the Long Pool all morning and by lunchtime this mighty pool was our own, and what's more was at a perfect fly-fishing height. I remember driving back to Grantown at lunchtime and still the snow was falling, it really was like a scene from a Christmas card!

After lunch we returned to the deserted Long Pool with George as optimistic as ever saying, 'Don't worry, Ian, we'll have a fish or two today, we will!' I must admit I was beginning to have my doubts, but comforted by George's encouragement, put a brave face on the somewhat arctic conditions and back into the water we went. We were both fishing with sink-tip lines and George had introduced me to his all-time favourite spring fly which at first sight seemed rather way out on colour! The fly is, in fact, completely purple and is tied in a number of variations, (see photo page 37) but for our purposes today we were fishing the fly tied on a 2-in Waddington shank. George has fished with this fly for a number of years now and since taking a fresh fish on the opening day in February 1991 rarely fishes any other pattern. 'What do you call it, George?' 'Very good,' he replied, grinning from ear to ear. Somehow I couldn't help thinking of that wonderful Jimi Hendrix number Purple Haze dating way back from the Swinging Sixties! I turned to George and said, 'That's it: Purple Hays' using the first three letters of George's surname. It seemed appropriate, George laughed but approved thoroughly of the name and so we both made our way towards the water. The river as yet hadn't risen much and by now the snow was beginning to ease. Slowly my confidence was beginning to rise.

Just after 3 pm and with the sky beginning to clear a little, we were joined by another angler who became involved in conversation with George about the weather, would you believe! I was fishing about halfway down the pool and at this point the flow seemed to

Purple Hays – in various sizes.

slow considerably and I was therefore having to slowly hand-retrieve the fly back towards me. I had made a cast and just started to hand-line when I felt a sudden pull as the fly swung in to the dangle, so I lifted and tightened but to no avail, it was indeed the briefest of encounters. I felt robbed, especially after enduring such blizzard-like conditions! I was fairly sure it was a salmon, but of course, it might well have been one of these early sea-trout.

I walked back up the bank to George and told him of this latest occurrence, which at least gave us some encouragement. George was keen to fish the tail of the pool before tea-time so I said I would follow him down. At this height (2-ft on the gauge) the tail picks up speed again and although not deep the fly fishes perfectly. It was about 4.30 pm when I spotted a lovely fish way down at the very tail and called, 'Just above the rough water, George.' He turned and called back, 'We'll have him,' with a beam on his face. I remember thinking as I looked up at the sky how the light had suddenly changed, sunlight was once again showing through the high white clouds, the air temperature had lifted and now it felt like a good fishing day. Then I heard George's reel scream way below me and a mighty fish erupted into the air. 'Well done, George,' I cried. Fishing this tail involves a long wade and, therefore, extra care must be taken when playing a fish, as wading back to the bank can be somewhat hazardous. Soon we were both back on terra firma and I made my way back to George with the net. This fish had given some fantastic sport, but as it tired we found a small bay and I was able carefully to slip the net under the fish and lift it on to the bank. It was one of those lovely Spey spring salmon, short and deep and weighing 18lb, an absolute corker. The Purple Hays was well and truly imbedded into the scissors. George was delighted and declared, 'We'll have some more this evening, Ian, just you wait and see!' After an early supper we returned with Wendy to find one or two more anglers had decided to venture out for the evening. There was great excitement from our fellow anglers and talk of many fish being seen, one hooked there, one lost over the other side, my adrenaline was beginning to flow! George went to the head of the pool and so I decided to follow Wendy down to the tail. Conditions looked ideal but I decided on a change of fly and went back to my old favourite black and yellow Aros tube.

Wendy had only been fishing a short while when she was into a fish and a fellow angler had already gone to her assistance. Just then there was a fast pull on my line and I too had hooked a fish, quite incredible, two fish on at the same time. I made my way to the bank and as Wendy and I both played our fish the chap with the net couldn't decide who to help first! I told him to help Wendy and fortunately I was able to beach my fish which turned out to be a cracking sea-trout of 2½lb. Wendy's fish was a lovely brown trout of about 2lb. It was a brilliant start to the evening and expectations were running high. I managed to pull another fish soon after, but suddenly, as quickly as the pool had come alive it went dead.

As the light began to fade my hopes began to lift as this is my very favourite time of the day. Many people had left to warm themselves with a soothing dram or two but I decided mine would wait. It was just before 10 pm and I had changed back onto George's Purple Hays. The long 2-in Waddington looked excellent in the water and having seen George's performance earlier in the day I was now fishing with more confidence. It was beginning to turn colder and by now I was right down to the very tail and had waded a long way out. The fly fished well and there was no sign of snagging rocks as I approached the shallows. I was just thinking it was nearly time to

George Haywood with a magnificient 18-lb salmon caught on a Purple Hays Waddington off the Long Pool, River Spey.

call it a day when the fly swung back towards the dangle, was seized viciously and nearly pulled my arm out of its socket, followed by the longest scream of the reel – quite magnificent! I looked around to see the bank which appeared to be miles away. Slowly and carefully I made my way back, inching my feet over the rocks, the fish made some long energetic runs towards the rough water, but luckily I was able to hold and turn him. In what seemed like an age I had made my way back onto the bank only to find George waiting with the net; he had heard the reel scream a hundred yards above me! The other few remaining anglers had by now gathered round. I found another small bay and carefully brought the fish round as George put the net under the fish and out on the bank lay a magnificent, gleaming bar of fresh-run silver sea-trout weighing exactly 7lb. It was a magnificent fish and greatly admired by my team of onlookers. Once again, the Purple Hays was well back into the scissors and George turned to me and said, 'I told you we'd have a fish tonight!'

The next day saw temperatures lift followed by the mother of all floods, bringing the Spey up by some 4½ feet and turning it into a muddy torrent. As the snow melted from the Cairngorms and surrounding hills fly-fishing was hopeless, although the worm fishers had an absolute field-day all over the entire stretch of the Association Water. By Wednesday it had started to fall and clear, my last day before heading south. It was still a big river, however, and wading was tricky. I had changed onto a Wet-Cel 2 sinking line #11 which seemed ideal in these astonishing

A large spring salmon and a beautiful early-run sea trout of 7lb: both caught on the irresistible Purple Hays Waddington.

This sea trout took the Purple Hays viciously and was hooked well back in the scissors.

conditions for the middle of May. Once again it was the evening which brought success for me. At about 8 pm I took a super clean cock salmon of 8lb on my black and orange 1-in Aros tube. I decided to change back to the Purple Hays just before dark; this time I was following George down and in the gloaming I saw a quiet head and tail movement just below me and opposite George. I called quietly and indicated my sighting. One more cast and I was over the fish and again another screaming take indicated my second fish of the evening, yet another superb sea-trout of 3½lb which had submitted to the attraction of the Purple Hays!

George and Wendy fish with this fly throughout the spring and summer months and have great success fishing for sea-trout during those short June nights tied on small Esmond Drury trebles. The fly dressings are as follows:

Silver Waddington: Body – flat silver, rib – oval silver tinsel, wings – purple buck-tail top and bottom, cheeks – jungle cock, head hackle – purple cock.

Palmered Waddington: Body – purple ostrich herl, hackle body – purple cock, rib – oval silver tinsel, wings – purple buck-tail top and bottom, cheeks – jungle cock, head hackle – purple cock.

Silver trebles: tied on Esmond Drury trebles size 8–16, tail – purple squirrel tail, body – flat silver, rib – silver oval tinsel, head hackle – purple cock.

Palmered treble: 8–16, tail – purple squirrel tail, body – purple ostrich herl, rib – silver oval tinsel, head hackle – purple cock.

It always seemed odd to me when I lived north of the Border, that anyone should ever think of going south for salmon fishing. For that reason the Wye never really appealed to me and it certainly seemed out of character when compared with Scotland's delightful, streamy waters.

However, a friend bought a first-class middle-Wye beat and invited us for a weekend's fishing saying: 'Come in the spring, Ian, and you might just catch one of those Wye 40-pounders!' It was an appealing thought. I had often seen photographs of those mighty Wye 'portmanteaux'.

Thus it was on a Thursday afternoon late in May, Annie and I went to Herefordshire to spend a long weekend with Michael at his lodge, nestling in a delightful wooded setting with a magnificent view over the river.

Having spoken to Gerry, the gillie, on the phone at lunchtime, we were feeling optimistic as we drove west along the M4. Gerry had told us the river was just 3ft on the gauge and starting to fall off after nearly three days of heavy rain. The water, however, was quite coloured and would probably not be suitable for fly-fishing. Sightings lower down had been of huge numbers of salmon waiting to run – what more could we wish for?

Holme Lacy, The Golden Mile, River Wye, Herefordshire. The sun sets over the Boat Pool as two swans settle on a crib (man-made – also known as croys to most of us). They were designed to give extra flow in the slower water and provide facilities to let fish rest and pause on their upstream journey.

Michael Leather fishing the Boat Pool at Holme Lacy in early spring. Although the river here is wide, fish tend to lie very close in to the point where he is standing and therefore only a short cast is needed to cover that lie.

We arrived at about 7.30 pm, so our fishing time was limited, but we hurriedly unpacked the car and tackled up with a couple of spinning rods and size 4 Mepps as suggested by Gerry. Annie had never caught a salmon, so, keen that she should have the best chance, I put her down the pool ahead of me. We had been fishing for about five minutes when Annie's rod bent into a lively salmon, the fish jumped a couple of times and she let it take line when it wanted to run. We had rehearsed this many times with the reel tension set to just the right setting, and she knew exactly what to do. After a further five minutes the fish was ready for the net. It was a lovely fresh 9½-pounder and a super first salmon – she was delighted, and we both admired her prize as it lay on the bank.

A few fish moved into the tail of the pool as the light started to fade, but we didn't have another offer, so it was back to the lodge for a large celebratory dram. When Michael arrived at 11 pm, he was delighted to see Annie's fish gleaming on the tray.

The next morning we were up bright and early. The water was just 3ft on the gauge, but still with quite a lot of colour in it. Michael, fishing down the Boat Pool with a Mepps, soon hooked another fresh fish of just under 9lb. With fish starting to show throughout the beat, the day looked promising, and the reports of a large run of fish moving up seemed to be confirmed. For all our efforts, however, we had no more offers that day.

On the Saturday morning, with the river falling slowly but still holding a lot of colour, coming largely from the River Lugg, Michael decided to give the worm a dunking. Now I was to see a method of worm fishing which employs a totally different type of tackle to that used in Scotland.

A 2- to 3-ft leader carrying the hook is attached to the line with a swivel. Above this is threaded a secondary swivel which runs freely, and attached to this with nylon a little less than the leader length is an Arlesley Bomb weight. The weight is varied according to water height and flow. Thus, if the water is fast and streamy, then the weight is heavy, while a lighter weight is used in slacker water. Getting the correct weight, so that the bait gently trundles downstream, is critical to success (see diagram 4).

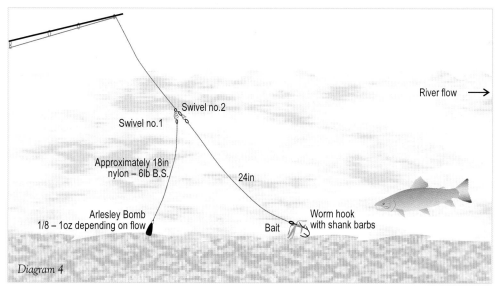

Diagram 4

Michael Leather has reason to look pleased with this beautiful fresh spring salmon of 21lb taken from Boat Pool, Holme Lacy, River Wye. The fish had shown in its lie and Michael had hooked it almost immediately. It was often a feature here – having seen a fish, especially in the spring, a well presented bait would more often than not result in its downfall!

Despite what some people say about worming, it is, when practised properly, an exciting method that is almost an art form. The contact felt when a fish gently mouths the worms is an unforgettable experience.

At lunchtime we found that Michael had taken another fish, this time a lovely sea-liced 12-pounder, and he had missed a third just before we arrived. We had seen several fish upstream, but none were interested in our various offerings.

After lunch Gerry went up to fish where we had been thrashing away all morning, and, of course, he returned at tea-time with another beautiful 11-pounder. By now I was feeling slightly concerned, I seemed to be in the wrong place at the wrong time, or was it the right place at the wrong time?

Michael and I determined on a different approach in the evening to see if we could do any good from the boat. The latter part of the day had seen a definite lack of fish showing – just one or two here and there which were probably resident and a couple in lies at the top of the beat which were inaccessible from the bank, but easily covered from the boat. As we rowed gently upstream, we saw fish starting to come in at the tail of the Boat Pool, and we should have abandoned the boat fishing exercise there and then; but hindsight is a wonderful thing!

Annie was fishing at The Planks as we rowed past, and I saw some fish 'veeing' their way through close to the bank. After an hour's fruitless fishing from the boat, we arrived back opposite Annie who had been joined by Michael's brother Robert, hot-foot from London. They told us that a lot of fish were showing, particularly one large fish which had been moving consistently for half an hour. Despite covering it several times, however, they had been unable to tempt it.

Annie was going back to fish the last half-hour in the Boat Pool, but Robert decided to carry on trying for the 'big one'. Within minutes his gold Mepps was seized and his rod bent double. Michael and I quickly went ashore to help him and, just before dark, and after a good, long fight, we netted a magnificent 12-pounder covered in sea-lice. The fish was beautifully shaped and it was amazing to see so many lice on it so far – 60 miles – from the sea. The fish were certainly getting a move on! Three fish for the day wasn't bad, but I was still blank, what would tomorrow bring?

Next morning Michael offered me first choice on the whole beat. It was a difficult decision, but as I pondered, a large fish showed just below us in the Boat Pool. 'That's it!' I said, 'The Boat Pool!' Tackling up with two large lobworms, I cast just above where the fish had shown and worked slowly down.

One of the incredible things about fishing here apparently is that if you see a fish show, then more often than not you will catch it. Usually it's the other way round: if you see a fish show, you seem never to catch it! Now, suddenly my line snagged – at just the right spot, too. I tried to free my bait by walking down the bank and giving several hefty jerks, muttering under my breath the while. Then, of course, the 'bottom' began to move and I was well and truly into a large and powerful fish which, after a long initial run, leapt into the air to show its glorious silver flanks in the early-morning sunshine. What a sight!

By now my catch had been seen by the others, and Michael was ready with the net. It was an epic battle. I seemed unable to tire the fish at all, indeed, if anyone was tiring, it was myself! Half an hour later, however, the fish was on its side and Michael slipped the net under it – a magnificent sea-liced 16-pounder. I was jubilant, what a way to start the day!

The day developed into a real scorcher. It was the first time we had seen sunshine during the weekend and the temperature was rising quickly by eleven o'clock, again we didn't see many fish move, and we had no more offers.

A small run of early grilse did come into the beat later that afternoon, and we decided to rest the water for a few hours and fish again when the sun was off, which we thought would offer our best chance.

Later on in the evening I went to the top of the beat, which until now had been too high to fish. Lucky Stone is a fast, streamy pool, and best suited to lower water. It is also an excellent fly water. However, although the height was down to about 2ft 6in, the water still carried some colour. Gerry said the ideal height for the pool was about 2ft for the fly and the fly was coming off the lies too quickly.

Then I fished the worm back down, and towards the tail of the run I felt that *knock, knock* which I knew only too well to be the tell-tale mouthing of a salmon. I gave him time and felt the *knock, knock* again. I was sure I had him and I tightened. He was a large fish and made some good, long runs, but I never saw him at all. Then, after another long run, the hook pulled out and he was off. Perhaps I hadn't given him enough time. Never mind! It had been an enjoyable few minutes and a second fish for the day would have been luck indeed.

Next morning, Sunday, which would have been a non-fishing day in Scotland, we awoke to another warm, sunny day. Michael said we should try the top pool again, which by now should be almost at perfect height. I fished the fly through on an intermediate line, but still I had no offer, and with fish showing in the headstream I thought the worm was worth another try.

First cast, right at the head of the run, I had a knock, and then the fish showed well above me and, *BANG*, he was on. I couldn't believe it, it was a really super take, followed by a long run as my rod bent over. After ten minutes of really hectic battling – this one was a real jumper and must have been in the air at least a dozen times – the fish was on its side and I drew it over Michael's waiting net, another lovely fresh fish of 12lb.

We fished on, but the day became another hot one and everything went quiet throughout the beat; however, it was a most impressive score for a weekend's sport, seven fresh fish taken from a river which I had never before considered fishing.

A 12-lb salmon caught by the author from Lucky Stone, Holme Lacy, River Wye. The fish fell to the worm and took the bait in one go, running and showing in the fast water, showing in the air at least a dozen times.

SUMMER ON THE KOLA – THE PONOI RIVER

'Be ready to leave for Russia on 10th May,' the voice on the other end of the phone said. Mariusz Wroblewski, manager of the Ponoi River Company, was calling from Helsinki, offering me the position as one of the fishing guides on the Ponoi River on Russia's Kola Peninsula for the forthcoming fishing season. To say I was excited was an understatement and if I remember rightly there was a feeling running through me akin to landing my first-ever salmon, the adrenalin was already beginning to flow!

The Ponoi River Company employ a pool of international guides from the United States of America, Canada, Russia and the United Kingdom to look after the needs of up to twenty clients a week at their Ryabaga Camp. The camp is situated some 225 miles south-east of Murmansk, high up in the Arctic Circle in a spectacular tundra wilderness. The river flows south and east into the Barents Sea through 300 miles of tundra, populated in its last 100 miles by only one small village of local reindeer herders and their families. The Ponoi has two main tributaries, the Purnache and the Atcha, which are also included in the fishing rotation and these are indeed rivers in their own right, looking very similar in size to many of the Scottish Highland rivers such as the Helmsdale, Brora and the Alness. Both are very productive, are reached by helicopter from the camp and always popular with all the fishing clients. It was a glorious, sunny spring day as we flew from Helsinki to Murmansk and then onward by helicopter some three hours into the Arctic wilderness. I say spring, but as we flew some 500m above the sparkling icy tundra below us, it became quite clear that winter was far from over. In time our first view of the Ponoi clearly showed a solid mass of ice bank to bank, moving slowly downstream and appearing from the air similar to a slow moving glacier. It was quite the most breathtaking sight I have ever seen in my life and I remember quickly thinking to myself, 'Neale, what on earth have you got yourself into now!' We landed on the helicopter pad just above our camp and took our first breath of clear, cold tundra air. It was truly a most wonderful feeling and at last we had arrived at what was to be our home for the next 5 months! We were duly introduced to our fellow Russian camp workers and guides and a team of some thirty to thirty-five people made up the full complement of the camp's staff.

During our first three weeks we were all allocated a daily routine of projects, which involved preparing and building up the camp in readiness for our first guests who were due to arrive at the end of the month. The camp consists of some 16 tents, all equipped with wood-burning stoves, vanity wash-basin and two single beds solely for guest accommodation. The main centre of the camp is the big tent which is used for dining purposes and equipped with wood-burning stove, fly-tying benches and a fully stocked bar! The camp also boasts shower block, sauna and flush toilets. The food is flown in fresh from Helsinki and Murmansk once a week, and prepared by a professional team of catering staff.

Kola days last twenty-four hours and the continuous daylight took some getting used to. However, after a day of building projects behind us we could at least look forward to attempting to cast a line, assuming we could find an ice-free zone!

Those early days were great fun and there was a real sense of pioneering as we explored and hunted out our new domain in an attempt to gain access to the river. I had become friendly with another Ponoi first-timer by the name of Mac McGee from Lookout Mountain in Tennessee. He and I both spent many of our evenings exploring the river as far as we could manage in those arctic conditions, which generally meant a long hike up river having waded through the ice-bound Ryabaga River, and then trudging through deep snow drifts until we could find access to some open river. This was made even more difficult as high banks of ice lay tight on the shore some three or four feet thick. Those first couple of weeks remained unseasonably cold, even for the Ponoi and water temperatures rarely lifted above 32°F. The air temperature at night would often fall to about 17–18°F. It was hard to believe that this river would be ready to accommodate fishing guests in just over three week's time, but miraculously it was! Looking back at my notes in my diary, we started catching our first fish from 18 May. These were all sea-trout and grayling. Many of these sea-trout were generally quite fresh and up to 2½lb in weight. Mac and I both fished our 15-ft salmon rods, mine with an intermediate line and 2-in black-and-yellow Waddington, while Mac fished a sink-tip line and a single hook size 2 Miramichi Special. All hooks are barbless and a maximum of a two-hook fly is permitted. When fishing with Waddingtons or treble hooks I would simply cut off one of the hooks with my pliers. The hooking potential was just as effective. The fishery rules are simple, barbless hooks and a catch-and-release policy is employed, however, a certain number of salmon are killed for scientific research and of course these fish are always welcomed by the kitchen to be served up at the dining table, either prepared as Gravlax, smoked or served oven-baked in foil and quite delicious of course.

I remember that first night so well, it was incredibly cold although the long walk through thigh-deep drifts did at least warm us. Our problem, of course, was trying to keep the rod guides free from ice, even my Marquis salmon reel started to freeze! However, we somehow or other managed to get a good length of line out casting between ice flows. The pace and flow of water was ideal and we could at least get good drifts with our flies. The sea-trout would generally follow the fly and occasionally bump it, followed by a long hard pull as the fly swung into the dangle. They were generally well hooked and playing a fish with frozen rod guides and reel was interesting to say the least! To be in such a beautiful wilderness, fishing in this totally unspoilt countryside was indeed heaven.

During the third week of May the weather began to show signs of improvement and at last the daily air temperatures were climbing into the low 40s°F, a heatwave by our standards. Suddenly the main bulk of ice above the Ryabaga Camp began to move and by Thursday 23 May we witnessed the most amazing sight. Hundreds of thousands of tons of ice began to move, breaking away from the banks. Huge rafts of white ice began to flow past our camp like ghosts in the night, the quietness was amazing with just the occasional bump as these blocks manoeuvred for position. We watched this spectacle for at least an hour and by now all our hopes were lifted and we felt sure that within a few days of this improving weather the main bulk of ice would be gone, and before long we would be able to get our boats afloat in readiness for our first arrivals. Within three days the weather and conditions had improved dramatically. The air temperature reached a staggering 54°F, the water temperature climbed to 39°F, and a feeling of spring was definitely in the air. However, large ice floes were still present and so bank fishing was our only way of practical fishing. With the melting ice, of course, the river was also beginning to rise and had come up 6–8in already. It was only a question of time now before the effects of melting snow and ice sponged through the tundra some 100 miles above us and brought the river up into an 8-ft flood. Until that time it would certainly not be safe enough to put the boats into the water.

However, on this particular fine Sunday evening it was a time to be fishing for salmon. This is where the salmon fishing on the Ponoi becomes so incredibly interesting and quite different from our own salmon rivers in the United Kingdom. Here on the Kola Peninsula we have another race of *Salmo salar*. Many salmon here enter the river during the previous autumn and overwinter in the river under the ice without spawning until the following autumn. They will then drop back as well-mended kelts the following spring, having spent the best part of eighteen months within the river system before returning to their sea-feeding habitat!

So here we have a unique river system which in the spring already has a large stock of salmon, having spent the winter months in deep winter holes and virtually in a state of hibernation. These fish are generally in the order of 10–18lb and seem to lose very little weight and remain incredibly bright! In fact, so good is the condition of these fish it is often very difficult to discriminate between a fall-run overwintered fish and fresh-run spring salmon which also begin to enter the river during the months of May and June. One easy way of identifying these fish is a close inspection of the gills, which will reveal fresh water gill parasites on the overwintered race. We even caught a number of 'grilse sized' salmon in those early days that had clearly overwintered as well! These fish were generally in the order of 6lb and I wonder if these would be classified as grilse or small salmon – scale information will give us the answers.

So let me go back to this particular Sunday in May. Mac had taken himself off upstream to our usual beat, whilst I stayed back in the camp to catch up making notes for this particular chapter! He had only been gone for about an hour and

The first two overwintered Ponoi salmon to be caught by Mac and Ian in May weighing 12 and 11lb. These salmon ran the river in the previous autumn to overwinter under the ice and spawn the following year. Note, however, these fish still retain their silvery appearance until water temperatures begin to rise.

returned back to the camp with a smile from Ponoi to Tennessee. 'Look at this Ian, my first Ponoi Atlantic salmon.' This was followed by a blood curdling 'YEE-HA' of excitement, which I am sure was almost heard back in Tennessee! Sure enough, he had caught a magnificent silver overwintered fish of just over 12lb. It was so deep, a classic example of an Atlantic salmon, I couldn't believe it, and we were all delighted as our colleagues emerged to witness the first salmon of the season caught off the Ponoi River. Now the season really had started!

In fact, so keen was Mac that he insisted that we go back up there and fish it again. 'I pulled another two fish and lost one,' he said. 'It's just come alive up there!' So just before midnight with the sun still shining bright, I wadered up and was ready to go. We made the long walk back, Mac placed me in his hot-spot, and I began to cast. Oh, what a joy to be able to fish without the rod guides getting iced up, this was bliss and the adrenalin was flowing! Within five or six casts I had a solid pull, lifted, it was on and then off. 'Keep going, Ian, it's full of fish in here,' Mac said, and sure enough within another few minutes my intermediate line with large black-and-yellow Waddington was suddenly intercepted and the fly just appeared to stop. I lifted the rod carefully and then felt the full weight of my fish as it took off across the Ponoi River like a missile. This was incredible, and before long I was able to beach and hand-tail the fish ashore, another fighting fit bright cock fish of just over 11lb, my first ever Ponoi salmon and caught just a little before 1 am. What a great feeling it was. As the week progressed so did the weather, with air temperatures stable in the mid-40s and the water temperature remaining steady at 38°F. The combination of both was enough to keep the main ice further up river breaking away from its winter grip. Over the course of the next day or so the river began to rise steadily into flood and after a couple of days it was soon safe enough to place the boats into the river and the chance for a couple of days' test fishing presented itself before our guests arrived!

All of the fishing over the 70-mile stretch is reached by boat or helicopter with ten different beats on the water. Two guests rotate daily onto a new beat with their guide. The river is generally very wide, often over twice the width of the River Tay, but surprisingly shallow and with a distinct peaty colour very similar to the River Spey in Scotland. The boats are sturdy flat-bottomed 18-ft aluminium and are powered by 55hp jet outboard motors, which are needed to cover the distances between beats. Although the Ponoi offers excellent bank fishing many clients prefer the comfort and accessibility of boat fishing. The procedure is simple, with one rod fishing from the stern and the other rod fishing from the bow on the boat's other side. Because of the fast-flowing nature of the rivers, the anchors are heavy (they weigh some 25 kilos). Raising and lowering them is superb exercise for chest expansion and arm muscle development! We usually fished by dropping the boat steadily down from an anchored position, often using a rope of up to 200ft in length. In the early days of May and June with the high water conditions the general rule is to fish close to the bank where the river pace is slow enough to offer a good drift for the fly, and as with all aspects of spring fishing it often pays to fish deeper and slower.

By the end of May we had completed our projects in the camp and once the boats were out we could then erect the lunch tents on each beat, which are equipped with tables, chairs and log-burning stove for those inclement Russian summer days!

Within the next couple of weeks, we had all settled into our daily routine of guiding our guests on what can only be described as the best Atlantic salmon river in the world. June is a prime month and sport was quite incredible, one week alone saw a total of some 1400 salmon landed to just 20 rods! The Ponoi salmon are by far the most aggressive fish I have ever seen and will readily come to a fly time and time again, providing it hasn't been pricked of course. We would often work a fish by changing fly size or colour before finally getting the salmon to take. This was always interesting and a thrill once the winning formula had been found. Another fascinating aspect of their behaviour is the jumping fish syndrome – more often than not the rule here is see a fish jump, cover it and catch it! Fly patterns vary enormously here and there is no one pattern which could be considered better than others. However, the one common factor, generally, is in the size. Big singles, doubles and tube-flies with long trailing fibres are ideal, such as the Ally's Shrimp patterns. Other popular patterns include Green Highlander, Ponoi Red, Garry Dog, Thunder

and Lightning, Mickey Finn and the Black Sheep patterns. As water temperatures began to rise and climb into the mid-40s° F, the fish would rise to a fly on floating line. Therefore, sink-tip and intermediate lines could be put away. In fact, many guests were taking fish on floating lines during the first week of operations. We had some wonderful sport during those early June weeks with floating lines and large flies, with fish often boiling and bulging at the fly, sometimes chasing eagerly as the fly swung round into the dangle. An angler here too keen to strike will simply pull the fly out of the fish's mouth.

Now was the time to start fishing the dry fly, something I had always longed to do for salmon. The most effective dry fly patterns are the 'bomber' type or muddler minnows. All of these are tied with one essential common

The author holds a fine fresh salmon caught by one of his clients on the Ponoi, just prior to tagging and returning the fish to the river.

A selection of dry-fly 'Bombers' used to great effect on the Ponoi as soon as the water temperature begins to lift into the mid 40s °F. Salmon will rise eagerly to a hitched Bomber skated across the surface.

ingredient designed to keep the fly well afloat and, of course, that's the use of deer hair. Unlike the muddler with just a head of deer hair, bombers are designed with a full hook length of bulky deer hair of varying colour and a sparse palmered hackle to give the extra attractiveness. These flies are designed to be floated across the stream to create a large 'V' or a wake on the surface. There are quite a number of clients who are totally addicted to dry-fly fishing. They will often not even consider fishing a conventional wet fly and I can see why. The whole procedure of fishing 'dry' is quite mesmerising, rather like dapping in a Scottish or Irish loch. There is an enormous degree of skill and concentration required, to see these fish eagerly pursue the fly with such aggression is quite astonishing. I will never forget my first 'dry' fish on an orange-and-white bomber pattern as it came for the fly some five times before it actually took hold, and then all hell let loose. Eventually, a slightly coloured cock fish of about 10lb was netted, followed by another two salmon in fairly quick succession!

Another interesting method here is the use of a simple half-hitch knot which is used by many anglers on the dry fly method. The half-hitch is tied in just behind the eye of the hook and this knot allows the fly to stay up high on the surface 'riffling' as it swings across the current. This method is otherwise known as the 'Riffle Hitch'. Fishing the dry fly is interestingly almost an all-season method and we were rising salmon to the dry fly right up to the last week of the fishing season at the end of September, even when air and water temperatures had dropped quite considerably. However, I had noticed in these later days the fish would more often than not rise to the dry without actually taking hold. As with dapping and dibbling it would appear that the fly was causing a reaction to just look at the fly. Sometimes it would be a boil, at other times the fish would come up and hit the fly with its tail and turn back to its lie without even a chance of a take. On these occasions often a change back to a standard wet pattern would result in a more positive reaction and a solid take from the fish. Because of the aggressive nature of these Russian salmon, there was always more time to experiment with different fly patterns and techniques. I remember one particular evening when Mac and I went out for a couple of hours – Mac fished the dry fly only and would rise salmon to his bomber. I would watch and wait and then immediately cover these fish with a large Ally's Shrimp – always with the inevitable result – a solid 'humdinger' of a take. But it was always fun to see the fish rising like trout to an olive on a Hampshire chalkstream.

As I have already mentioned earlier the Ponoi River is regulated and controlled as a catch-and-release fishery. It is the only river on the Kola Peninsula designated by the Russians as a test river for Atlantic Salmon research as a joint Atlantic Salmon Federation (ASF)/PINRO long-term study project.

This research on behalf of the Atlantic Salmon Federation is headed by Dr Fred Whoriskey who is Vice President, Research and Environment for the ASF. He arrived in 1994 to begin a long-term project in collaboration with Russian scientists. With the opening of sport fishing in 1991 the Ponoi netting at the mouth of the river was reduced and then eliminated after the 1993 season. A large part of this research requires an organised salmon tagging programme. All guides are issued with tag guns and notebooks so that we are all able to assist Fred Whoriskey with this valuable research. Having caught a salmon, it will be tagged and quickly released back to the river. The tags are soft plastic strips (called Floy Spaghetti tags) and inserted into the fish just below the dorsal fin. Every tag is individually numbered for ident- ification purposes. We then record the date, time and place of capture, sex of the fish and the name of the captor. All this

The Ponoi River: Lower Tomba in summer showing off its stunning colours and scenery with a fine backdrop of the 'Falcon's Nest'.

information is then stored on Fred's computer back at the camp and gradually over the course of the season a large database of information is built up. The information and data that has been recorded shows some remarkable statistics and without doubt, it shows that the catch-and-release policy on a salmon fishery is extremely effective. During the 1996 season some 1,200 salmon were tagged and released. From this some interesting information has been recorded, in addition to our own tagging efforts another 17 salmon were also implanted with electronic radio tags, again under the careful scrutiny of Fred Whoriskey. These selected fish were carefully operated on and the tags inserted into the body cavity, after 24 hours of recovery they were released back into the river. They were monitored by Fred and his team on a daily basis, from a boat with tracking antenna. These fish could be studied individually, as each fish had its own identification code, tag and number. Remarkably all 17 fish survived the ordeal of being caught, operated on and returned safely back to their environment, where their movements and progress was recorded to the end of the season. In this very large river, the biologists tracked 16 of 17 Fish for 2 weeks and 15 of 17 for the entire season. The seventeenth fish may have ascended a tributary here we could not follow, or perhaps fallen to a predator.

The tagging operation is indeed a very important part of the research programme and gave us some quite remarkable information, especially with regard to the number of recaptures for instance, which were often a daily occurrence. One particular day I remember well was while fishing on the Kolmac beat with one of my clients who was wading from the shore. He hooked a magnificent fish of just over 12lb which ran off his line and way down on to his backing, in fact, for a while it looked as though the fish might have spooled him, such was the ensuing battle! The fish was in the air at least half a dozen times. As it came to the net I spotted the little plastic tag below its dorsal fin, took a note of its number and quickly returned this magnificent spring fish. I duly reported my finding to Fred and was later informed that Bruce, one of my guiding colleagues, had tagged that fish only the day before. Bruce remembered the fish well, which had been caught on the same beat and almost in the same lie from what I could gather. However, after tagging the salmon he had had difficulty in reviving the fish and as he let the fish go he remembered seeing the fish turn belly-up and despite following it downstream in the boat in an effort to rescue it, was convinced that the fish most probably had not survived. Therefore, his face was a picture when I told him about our epic battle with that very same lost fish! We had many recaptures and often the fish were taken some 20 or 30 miles downstream or some 20 to 30 miles upstream. The information from the tagging procedure is of vital importance and is steadily giving us a definite view that catch-and-release on a salmon fishery does work well indeed. It also lets the biologists estimate the sizes of the runs. In all the time I was on the Ponoi neither I nor my colleagues saw one dead salmon in the water. During the early spring weeks we also caught many tagged kelts having spawned from the previous season which again bears testimony to the survival rate of the catch-and-release programme being employed on the Ponoi River. Remarkably two fish that had been tagged in 1994 were recaptured in the 1996 season, returning for another spawning run. (See The Scientific Angle, page 61).

Going into the month of July we saw the first of the grilse. By all accounts this was one of the biggest runs of grilse ever recorded for the Ponoi River. As with their larger cousins, they would seize a salmon fly, large or small, with amazing aggression, often chasing and pulling at the tail fibres, making a would-be striker hit them too

Summer salmon and grilse enter the Ponoi in large numbers throughout July and August offering sport for all anglers fishing floating lines and small flies or Bombers. Whilst the Ponoi is primarily a 'catch and release' fishery, a small percentage of salmon are killed for the scientific research programme. Scale and chemical analysis is used to determine specific data of individual fish (see The Scientific Angle). These fish are also welcomed by the kitchen and enjoyed by clients and staff alike.

soon. This often resulted in a fish hooked and quickly lost. When hooked they frequently took to the air, cartwheeling and surface splashing. Sometimes the acrobatics freed them from the barbless hook. These beautiful fresh, silver torpedoes were exciting sport, especially for those fishing a single-handed rod of 9–10ft and say an 8 or 9 weight floating line. At this time there was also a steady run of fine fresh summer salmon averaging about 8lb. These appeared in the river in good numbers by late July. Summer rainfall was generally quite light, resulting in only two decent rises in water level through the months of July and August. As the river fell back to a lower level it actually took on more character, with more fishable streams, glides and riffles appearing across the entire system. The Ponoi at low flow is generally not a deep river, and with an average depth of some 3–4ft the scope for taking fish in the middle deeper lies became a better prospect. For us guides low flow conditions were the most challenging and rewarding. I like the way Bill Currie describes the Ponoi: 'Within a big river there often lie a multitude of micro-rivers, the whole experience is a journey into specifics. The vast river is still there, of course, and you get a great buzz from being a tiny speck in it, but the vastness no longer daunts you. It changes into individual streams with purling runs and glassy flats in them, glides bulging over rocks, headlands with currents angling off them rich in salmon lies.'

As we moved into mid-August the small birch leaves began to turn a yellow-gold, the days shortened and at last we had a night sky and bright stars. There was an anticipation of autumn in the air and a growing excitement of large fresh 'Fall' fish which would soon begin to run the river in large numbers to overwinter under the ice.

Then the impossible happened. For a few weeks, we experienced something of a Russian heatwave with daily air temperatures in the high 70s and a water temperature of 62°F. Fishing conditions were challenging, however; by the end of the month air temperatures fell away and the water temperature slipped back to a comfortable 55–56°F, making for ideal fishing. By now we were seeing good numbers of these fine, fresh, deep autumn salmon in all of our beats.

September brought rain. After several days of downpours the mighty Ponoi rose by some 3–4ft into a good sized flood. This we felt sure would send out its message into the Barents Sea, encouraging the bulk of autumn fish to run, and it certainly did! With the onset of the heavy rain and the general cooler weather conditions, water temperatures began to fall back into the mid-40s. However, the big run was by now well underway and whilst sink-tip and intermediate lines were very successful during

the high water conditions the salmon were still prepared to rise to a large bright fly on a floating line, especially as the water started to fall and clear. Another big run of sea-trout also made an appearance with some fine sea-liced specimens up to 3lb taken on salmon flies.

For me the whole season on the Ponoi was a fascinating experience, having worked with and enjoyed the company of my fellow guides and camp workers. I also made so many new friends and acquaintances from all parts of the globe, enjoying and sharing that one common passion that takes us to these far flung corners of the world – the sight of a boiling fish to the fly and that electric pull of the line as another king of kings is hooked. I have so many fond memories and the anticipation and excitement of another Ponoi season is already growing.

A happy client with her Russian guide Max, showing off a magnificent 18-lb autumn run salmon taken from the Purnache beat in September.

It had been a long and busy six weeks since the beginning of our Kola season on the Ponoi River. Catches had been record-breaking throughout June with an incredible one-week total of some 1,440 salmon to just 20 rods, giving an average of 73 fish per angler! We had been working flat out and were now able to look forward to some time off: time to relax, time to sleep and of course time to fish. After all, we were working and living on the most prolific Atlantic salmon river in the world.

'Let's make an early start,' I said to my 'roomy', Don Williams from British Columbia. We woke early to the sound of the breakfast bell clanging hard and soon made our way to the big dining tent to join our friends and guests to eat. It was a glorious mid-summer's morning with a gentle breeze blowing upstream from the Barents Sea. The conditions looked promising, and after the preparations had been made for our picnic lunch we were ready to go. We collected our fuel tanks and made our way to the jet boats moored just below the camp, it seemed odd to be walking down with our own rods for a change and we chatted excitedly about where we were going to start on our allocated beat some ten miles downstream. Once aboard, we were soon moving downstream as our 55hp jet motor creamed over the surface at high speed.

After the initial high snow and ice melt-water of June, when the river had risen by some 10ft, the water was now flowing at an ideal summer level and was incredibly clear. The water temperature was also ideal at 52°F, perfect for wet- and dry-fly fishing alike. As we travelled downstream we slowed under a rock face where a pair of Gyr falcons had nested and produced two fine chicks which were ready to fledge. They peered down at us some 20ft below and gave out high-pitched squeals together with much wing flapping. 'Not long to go now Don; I reckon they will be away within the week!' 'Come on let's go fishing – we only have today.' I agreed and we motored on.

By now the sun was high and barely a cloud was to be seen in the sky as we pushed into the top of our beat. Don and I like to fish from the bank – wading and exploring is always more exciting. We tethered our boat to the shore. 'I'll go up, Don and you start in here.' We were both fishing double-handed rods, mine being a 14-ft Bruce and Walker Powerlite with a DT 10 floating line, a 10lb BS leader and a size 8 Ally's Shrimp double – my all-round favourite combination. Don was fishing his 15-ft Loomis, a DT 11 Speycaster line and size 8 Silver Stoat double.

I saw one fish roll quietly by a rock. It made a half-hearted pull at the fly but would not come again. We both waded carefully down and searched hard for fish; by now the sun was full on the water and the glare was quite intense; already it was nearly mid-day and both of us were fishless. I decided to take a break and take some photographs of Don sending out over 100ft of fly line from a perfect double Spey cast. I called out and said, 'Just a 4-pounder for lunch Don!' He grinned and said, 'Okay, I've even brought the lemon!' We moved further down to a faster section of more oxygenated water. I changed over to a Jim Vincent Windcutter Spey line, which was effortless to cast. I was just approaching a rocky point, which breaks the flow with a fine riffle and always holds a few fish. Just above the point a head and tail broke surface – this surely was a taker? I made the cast and the Ally's was right on target. Sure enough, just at the right moment there was a pull followed by a series of pulls. The reel screamed and I lifted the rod. The fish took to the air in a series of cartwheels and within five minutes I was back on shore and able to beach a fine fresh grilse of around 4lb – covered in long-tailed sea-lice just fresh in from the Barents sea. Don called out a hearty yell, and I held my fish up for him to see. This was great to see and a sign of things to come, the grilse were beginning to run. Shortly after I rose another fish but it would not come again. Don by now had waded some way and he too had hooked a fish in midstream, a coloured hen fish that he quickly released. We decided to move on down and find a suitable place for lunch. Misha, one of my Russian friends, who fishing from a boat, pulled alongside and we learned he had taken two fish from either side of the big rock in Eagle pool, so we were now all seeing some action at last. 'Come and join us for lunch Misha', I said as I held up my fresh grilse. He grinned, 'Okay, I will be with you in half an hour.' We found a fine rocky bank, slightly shaded and out of the fresh upstream wind. We gathered together dry tinder and soon had a fire blazing. The smell of birch burning and the prospect of barbecued fresh run Salmon was quite appetising.

Luckily Don is not only an incredible fly-tyer and salmon fisher but also a fully qualified chef! He filleted the fish, added seasoning and finely chopped chives; the latter grow abundantly along the banks of this great river. These banks by mid-July are ablaze with the colours of wild flowers such as violet, dog-rose and red clover. It always amazes me that despite the soil being frozen for eight months of the year such a profusion of flowers appears in the short summer season.

Misha had caught another fine fresh grilse that was prepared and put with mine in an aluminium smoking bag. Once the embers were red hot the bag was placed into the fire for about fifteen minutes. The fish were cooked to perfection. Good fishing, good food and good company; who could ask for more? We were feeling happy with our lot in life, relaxing and chatting together on this day of days. Did you hear the story about the Russian, the Canadian and the Scotsman? Well, you know what I mean! Just at that point, a juvenile sea eagle appeared over us and drifted on the thermals over the treetops, and small songbirds of many varieties called out around us. The experience of this tundra wilderness is truly amazing; I felt privileged to be part of it all.

It was nearly 4 pm by the time lunch was finished. The sun still shone bright but shade was appearing on the far shore so we decided to travel across and fish that bank. Misha bade farewell and moved on downstream. Don fished below me and I walked up the rocky bank looking for promising runs and riffles. I spotted such a lie where midstream stones pushed the current toward a rocky outcrop on the bank, so creating a most enticing 'V'. I waded in carefully well above and started to lengthen line; as I did so a good fish jumped clear of the water. Now if you see a fish jump on the Ponoi, the chances are that you will catch it. Still fishing the Ally, I worked down toward the fish but nothing stirred, I wondered if he might have dropped back. The pull in the 'V' was perfect and the fly was fishing well. Just when I thought I had passed the lie it took with a savage pull and line shot from the reel. Don looked round and gave the thumbs up. It was a strong fish and fought hard; I landed the coloured cock fish of around 8lb and noticed a tag trailing from the base of its dorsal fin, I took a note of the number and carefully returned the fish to the water. It is always exciting to make a recapture, indicating that the catch-and-release system is effective and does little harm to the fish. I later learned that this fish was originally caught in early June from a pool some 10 miles down-river (Lower Tomba).

We both decided to move back upstream and explore one or two areas on this same side about a mile above. I went to check a large bend where the fast flow pulled in tight to our side then slowed into a tail of rocky runs and riffles. Don dropped me off and went back downstream some 300yd. I hadn't even put out a full length of line, when I had a really solid pull close to the shore – the fish must have been lying in less than 2ft of water. It took off, exploding across the Ponoi and I could see it was big and fresh. After a spectacular fight I beached a lovely hen fish of around 10lb. We often got a run of these big hen fish at the end of June or the beginning of July; possibly late spring or early summer fish. Every month of the season on Ponoi sees a run of fresh fish which is exciting. I returned my silver prize and moved down a little further. My confidence was running high and my senses were primed with anticipation.

The sun had edged over the hill and the cool shade felt good after a day of continuous heat. I also spotted one or two fish rolling and splashing in midstream, maybe I was standing over a run of fresh fish that were also enjoying the shade. However, there were two problems to contend with, the upstream breeze had developed into a force 5 and neat presentation was now difficult. The wade was very difficult but I persevered with a single Spey cast over my right shoulder. This run was also stiff with big grayling and after three follows they were becoming a nuisance. Another pull followed, 'Another grayling', I thought, so I began to speed up the fly by retrieving when on the dangle. A fish hit the fly hard and salmon number four was on, it was hooked right in the snout but stayed on. I landed a fresh hen fish of similar size to the last; it was covered in sea-lice and was just a picture. I was really in my element and hoping Don was having as much fun. I then saw a classic head and tail rise in easy casting range by a large rock. I covered it but it did not rise. I decided to work this fish, Ponoi fish are very aggressive and will often respond to a change of fly, either wet or dry. I put out a Munro killer size 8 and a fish boiled at the fly without touching. I tried again and third time came another boil and gentle pluck. 'Damn!' I thought, I had pricked him. Despite another change the fish was no longer interested. It had been a really hot hour; Don had also taken another and lost one – the Ponoi had started to bubble.

We moved further upstream to a popular area known as The Beach. This is a lovely piece of water with easy wading on a gravel bed. Don decided on a change of tactics by going for a large bushy Bomber dry-fly. The fish were obviously more active and the visual concept of dry-fly fishing was wonderful. Within minutes, as the fly waked over the surface, a nose showed and followed the fly, hitting it just before lift-off. Contact was brief, however, and the fish was gone. He rose two more fish without a take – they were beginning to get choosy again! We became aware of the falling air temperature and a glance at the watch showed 8.30 pm. I was feeling bushed but incredibly happy with life as I sat on the back of the boat and watched Don working down towards me. He could see I was ready for home, 'Well, what do you reckon Ian, maybe it's time for something to eat?' I was happy with the idea and we made our way back to camp. It had been a splendid day's fishing with seven salmon between us and plenty of activity. As I sunk a large dram back at camp, I was able to reflect on life and on the guides' day off, fishing on the best Atlantic salmon river in the world. What a life indeed!

THE SCIENTIFIC ANGLE

The Ponoi River system is situated within the Kola peninsula in northern Russia on the eastern tip of the same tongue of land that gives rise to Norway, Sweden and Finland. The river flows in an easterly direction to meet the Barents Sea on the eastern tip of the peninsula just north of the Arctic Circle. Being remote from industrialisation and being largely inaccessible, except by helicopter, its waters are clean and free from effluents. There are no natural or man-made obstacles to fish migration and thus this river system offers a perfect environment for the Atlantic salmon. This region remains one of the last unspoiled wildernesses in the world.

In addition to offering spectacular fly-fishing for Atlantic salmon, this river offers the perfect opportunity for a study of fish biology. Furthermore, it allows a scientific assessment of the impact of such sport fishing on salmon behaviour in the wild. The Ponoi system is particularly amenable to such studies for three main reasons. Firstly, there is currently no commercial netting carried out in the river or at its estuary. Secondly, this is a prolific salmon river; many thousands of fish are caught and returned each year and this allows statistical assessments to achieve significance. Finally, the access to fishing is solely through Frontiers Inc. and the Ponoi River Company whose guests and guides are all based in one camp on the main river. This allows the scientific programme to be well organised throughout the system, with virtually 100% returns on reports of tagged fish caught.

A collective commercial fishery did operate on the Ponoi until 1993 by blocking the river with a barrier fence. In effect, one of every two salmon entering the river was taken but fishery managers were responsible for monitoring fish stocks closely. The Russian government closed commercial fisheries in 1993 in order to promote sport fishing, a decision which is bound to have major implications on the salmon population in the river thereafter.

The Ponoi River Project was started in 1994. It is a co-operative effort of the Atlantic Salmon Federation, the Knipovitch Polar Research Institute for Marine Fisheries and Oceanography (PINRO) and the Ponoi River Company. The aim of the programme is to conduct scientific research which will permit a better understanding, and hence management, of Atlantic salmon on the Ponoi River and perhaps worldwide. Financial support for the programme comes from the Ponoi River Company, the National Fish and Wildlife Foundation, the Trust for Mutual Understanding and private donors. Without such sponsorship the scientific programme would not exist.

The Ponoi River has two distinct salmon runs. The spring run fish arrive in June and July and spawn that autumn. The autumn fish, however, arrive from mid-August and continue up river under the ice which forms in October; this persists throughout the long winter until thawing the following May. These fish do not spawn in the year they arrive but do so the following autumn. They then overwinter again before returning to sea the following year. In effect they have overwintered twice and return to the sea up to twenty months after they first arrive. There is no evidence that such fish feed in the river and so they undertake a two-year fast for the sake of spawning! The two distinct fish populations, therefore, have very different biological characteristics. There must be sound biological or evolutionary mechanisms which drive this adaptation. The Ponoi River Project must consider these two salmon populations separately when behavioural and survival characteristics are being studied. We should also remember that an autumn fish might be caught in good condition in the year after it first entered the river. The fish is not a kelt as it has not yet spawned; it remains in good condition despite a year-long fast. How can this be so? Perhaps the autumn run fish have a distinctive diet rich in fatty acids with high calorific value which helps sustain them through the long fast. Perhaps the low water temperatures (compared to British rivers) allow a metabolic slowdown with consequent energy conservation. If this were so we might expect the autumn fish to remain dormant in the cold deeper pools of the river, and be unwilling to come to the fly. This is almost certainly not the case. In fact the Ponoi fish are far more likely to chase a fly, in particular a dry-fly, than their British cousins! We have much to learn about the biology of Atlantic salmon throughout the world. The unique behaviour of Ponoi fish generates a whole new series of scientific questions that we might never have previously considered. In 1996 the Ponoi River Science Program addressed a number of topics, the findings of which I shall summarise below.

Adult Salmon Population Estimates

The commercial salmon fishery on the Ponoi, which operated until 1993, took significant numbers of fish from the river system. In effect, every single fish entering the river was trapped and every other fish was killed, with the remainder being returned to maintain the population. Such a practice raises a few eyebrows but at least the fishery had the sense to monitor adult fish numbers with a view to adjusting the proportion of fish being taken. Clearly if the number of returning fish is falling consistently, one should kill fewer salmon in order for the indigenous population to recover. Although the circumstances are different in Britain i.e. multiple independent fisheries, incomplete harvesting of the crop, etc. this is a sound scientific principle which many commercial fisheries have failed to realise in the past (notable exceptions are the rivers Helmsdale, Naver, Thurso and Beauly in Scotland, where netting operations are directed by a single company who have sport fishing interests at heart).

Since the closure of this fishery alternative methods for assessing the adult salmon population need to be employed. The Ponoi River Project used an ingenious method, the Peterson estimate, for calculating the adult salmon population in 1996. Separate calculations were needed for spring run fish, kelts and autumn run fish as each behaves differently. However, there were not enough recaptures to calculate population estimates for each group and so the results were pooled. The basic principle is as follows: a number of salmon were caught during a specified fishing period and were marked using Floy spaghetti tags at the base of the dorsal fin and were released alive. Now the fraction of those fish which are recaptured, assuming a fish will take as freely a second time, is the same as the fraction derived from fish caught initially, divided by the total salmon population.

$$\frac{\text{Number of salmon caught first time M}}{\text{Total salmon population N}} = \frac{\text{Number of recaptures R}}{\text{Total fish caught in recapture period C}}$$

As three of these variables are known, the fourth i.e. the total salmon population (N) can be estimated. As the autumn fish continued to arrive long after the camp was closed in September a population estimate could not be accurately made. An exploitation rate was derived instead which indicates the number of fish in the section of river being fished, which were theoretically available to be caught. If such an estimate is made annually then the salmon population can be monitored from year to year.

By using such methodology it was possible to calculate that guided anglers caught around 10% of fish available in the river and that between 2 June and 9 August at any one time around 37,000 fish were present in the water being fished. This compares favourably with figures from 1994 but will be of great value in the future as trends are followed with time.

Recapture Patterns of Tagged Fish

One hundred and thirty-three tagged fish were recaptured during the 1996 fishing season. The average time between marking and recapture was 32 days; some, however, were of fish initially caught the previous year (which had not spawned) whilst two caught in 1994 had spawned and were running the river a second time. It is of interest that three fish were recaptured on the same day! Five of the fish tagged in 1996 were recaptured a second time and had thus been caught for a third time. Contrary to what one might expect fish could have moved upstream, downstream or stayed in the same beat at the time of recapture. More fish had moved downstream than up. So much for our understanding of salmon movement in rivers!

Catch-and-Release Work

In addition to the Floy tagging work noted above, a number of fish had radio tags implanted to accurately monitor fish movement. Autumn run overwintered fish captured by anglers were held in cages for 24 hours then anaesthetised whilst radio tags were surgically implanted in the abdomen. No fish died during surgery. After release, movement patterns were monitored using hand-held radio receivers from a boat covering the Ponoi main stem. Only one of 17 fish radio-tagged was never relocated. The remainder were tracked until the end of the season and two were even caught by anglers! Both appeared healthy and had fully recovered from the surgery.

Previous work has shown that the major mortality of fish caught on rod and line occurs within the first 24 hours after capture. All fish which were intended for tagging, were therefore kept in the river in cages for a minimum of 24 hours. Only one of the 62 fish held in this way died (98% survival). One assumes that the mortality would be higher had barbless fly hooks not been used. A similar proportion of Floy tagged (7.2%) and radio tagged (12%) fish were recaptured suggesting that an anaesthetic and radio tag implantation had no adverse effect on sporting behaviour.

Energetics of Autumn-Run Fish

Eleven of the radio tags allowed body temperature monitoring of the fish after release. This was compared with river water temperature over time using a probe set in the home pool of the Ponoi. Contrary to our hypothesis, the monitored fish appeared to relocate at sites of higher temperature than the point of reference. Although the method is subject to bias due to fish moving away from the reference probe (up or downstream or into a tributary) the findings were highly significant. On the basis of this limited study, the autumn run fish do not appear to conserve energy by remaining in the colder parts of the river.

Parr Studies

Parr surveys were undertaken on the Ponoi main stem and on a number of tributaries. Parr densities were calculated by electro-fishing for controlled periods of time over predetermined volumes of water in either riffles or flats. The parr were measured, sexed and aged using scale sampling and the data compared with that available from 1994, the year after the closure of the commercial fishery.

Virtually all areas sampled showed increases in parr and fry density compared with 1994; it is tempting to attribute this to the closure of the commercial fishery. One might anticipate that such an increase would occur at the expense of parr size and maturity due to the availability of food but this was not confirmed when data was analysed from these years. Such findings indicate that the salmon population is on the increase with an abundance of small fish; one hopes this will be confirmed with increasing numbers of adult fish returning in years to come.

Let us hope that the good work of the Ponoi River program can further our scientific understanding of this fascinating creature such that its survival is guaranteed, and that sport fishing might continue to be enjoyed in parallel. Such meticulous scientific study is likely to be of benefit, not just on the fabulous Ponoi River, but also on other salmon rivers throughout the world.

Acknowledgement
I am grateful to the Ponoi River Program, in particular Dr F. G. Whoriskey and Sergei Prusov (PINRO), for allowing access to the results of their work during the 1996 season.

A deep, fresh-run salmon from the Ponoi – these beautiful fish begin to appear in mid-August, with the main surge developing during September.

CHAPTER 5

JUNE
SEA-TROUT AT NIGHT, SALMON AT DAWN

'Hi, Neale! Listen, David's got to go back to town on business tonight. Can you get up to fish his rod?'

It was late June and Bill Currie's telephone call, when all the salmon rivers were showing their bones, seemed to offer an opportunity not to be missed. The sea-trout were coming into the river in great numbers, he told me, making their way upstream overnight and slipping into the loch above, probably never to be seen again in that heatwave summer!

Some really good fish had been taken on preceding evenings and Bill had caught one of just under 6½lb the night before, so prospects looked promising. Two hours later I had loaded the car and was on my way, arriving at the cottage in time for an early-evening inspection of our beat. I had never fished the river before and Bill was keen for me to see all the pools, the likely lies and the bank in daylight, so that I knew exactly the geography of the river; but it is difficult to memorise everything

The River Shiel. A classic example of a typical west coast salmon and sea-trout river, draining from Loch Shiel some 17½ miles long and into the river which is only 3 miles long.

The River Shiel, The Garden Pool. Many of the pools are quite slow and canal-like with difficult bank access especially during such low water conditions – therefore many wooden platforms have been built projecting into these pools offering the angler easier access for fishing.

quickly and a river-bank can feel very different in the dark compared with daylight.

A careful survey of all the likely hot-spots on the stretches we would be fishing after dark confirmed that Bill was right. The river was alive with fish and every now and then a huge silver shape would throw itself clear of the water, tempting us that little bit more. It was vital not to disturb these fish, so back to the cottage we went to tackle-up and have a wee dram before returning to the river to wait for darkness. It was a perfect evening: warm, plenty of cloud cover, and a good strong breeze to keep the bloodthirsty midges at bay!

Bill suggested I should fish the upper pool first, where we had seen some large fish showing earlier on; he would go downstream.

I started in at the head and slowly worked my way down the long, slow-moving pool. I had chosen a ½-in black-and-orange hairwing tube-fly for the point, with a Dark Mackerel single, size 8, on the dropper. I also fished a #6 slow-sink line on my Bruce and Walker 11ft 3in Century. This really is a versatile rod which can handle large sea-trout and grilse without problem. I have even caught an 18lb salmon on it, but that's another story! Bill fishes the same model in the slightly stiffer grilse version. It is a little too heavy for trout, but probably has the edge on my rod for salmon.

As I slowly covered every inch of fishable water, fish started crashing out of the water all around me and the excitement started to mount. Suddenly I felt a vicious pull – but it was gone in an instant. Then the same thing happened again. 'What's wrong with these fish?' I thought. At last, just before the tail of the pool – *Bang!* Halfway round I was into a good sea-trout.

What a great feeling it is to be connected to a powerful fish in the pitch blackness of night! I played the fish for several minutes and was just wondering where to land it when, for no apparent reason, the hooks pulled out. Normally the size 14 trebles stay in once they take hold, but not this time. I checked all three hooks and found they were still pin sharp.

It is always a good idea to check your hooks every now and then, especially in the dark. They may have hit a rock or other obstacle and lost their edge without your realising it and nothing is more infuriating than to hook a good fish only to have the hooks come out because the points are blunt.

Now I felt dejected, time was ticking on. It was 1.30 am and a midsummer night in north-west Scotland is not long. You have to make the most of your opportunities in a short time. Suddenly Bill emerged from the darkness, he had found a pool below crammed with fresh fish and had taken two reasonable sea-trout of 2lb apiece and lost another two. Sport was obviously brisk and he invited me to join him.

Bill positioned me in a likely spot and went further downstream to fish off one of the platforms. In a matter of minutes I heard his reel scream to signal fish number three.

Bill was fishing a neutral-density line with a ½-in Dark Mackerel Waddington on the point and it was this that was doing the damage. Now, when I fish with him for sea-trout I don't need to ask what fly he is using, I think it should be renamed the Currie Mackerel! On this occasion I decided to stick with my favourite tube-fly. If it could catch fish for me on my home ground, it was jolly well going to catch fish for me here!

I carried on fishing and my second cast had a fantastic take from a fish that really gave a good account of itself. It sped upstream, then down, following this with three acrobatic leaps; but I felt I was in control and enjoyed every minute of it. A few minutes later the fish came to the net, covered in sea-lice and just over 2lb. It was a perfect example of a west-coast sea-trout, with a tiny head and a short, deep body – and it had taken my tube-fly on the point! I heard a cheer of congratulation from Bill and then he was into number four. This one really made Bill's rod work, and I remember thinking at the time that it was no small fish. It certainly wasn't. It weighed a superb 3½lb. The pool was now alive with fish, fresh off the high tide at about midnight as we were only about a mile from the sea.

I cast across again, started a slow retrieve and almost at once the fly was grabbed by a perfect twin to my first fish. By now we had only about an hour of darkness left, but in that last hour I managed to take another four sea-trout from 1¼ to 1¾lb. I hadn't met one of those 6lb-plus beauties I had heard so much about, but I had a basket of six cracking sea-trout up to 2lb – a perfect size for eating – and had enjoyed a memorable night's fishing. I'd caught half-a-dozen finnock which had been carefully returned to fight another night.

Bill had moved up river as dawn approached, and his score then was eight sea-trout, mostly of similar size to mine. It was about 4 am when he returned without having added to his tally. 'Come on, Neale,' he said with a huge yawn, 'It's time to hit the sack!' What he didn't know was that in the half-light I had just seen a lovely head-and-tail rise of what I thought was a salmon on the far side of the pool. 'Hang on a minute, Bill', I said, 'One more cast!' Edging towards the lie, I cast and, sure enough, at the exact spot I'd seen the fish move I felt a gentle pull which I knew only too well was from a salmon. 'I pulled him, Bill!' I said. Bill actually stopped yawning at this point and began to look interested! 'Once more!' I said. This time, as I was leading the flies round about a yard further up, I felt another long, slow pull. 'Blast!' I said, 'That was him again!' Bill was by now wide awake and changing his point fly to a low-water size 8 Willie Gunn double. 'All right, Neale! You've had your chance! It's my turn now!'

Bill started casting, working his flies across and down to the same lie. Within a couple of minutes and in exactly the same spot, he was into the fish. By now I was feeling rather miffed, and I made one or two rather scathing remarks about my host as I put my net under a beautiful grilse of 6½lb, just off the tide and smothered in sea-lice.

Again Bill decided it was time for some shut-eye. 'He's getting old!' I thought. 'Poor chap!' I didn't tell him I'd spotted another head-and-tail! I changed to the favoured Willie Gunn and cast towards the lie, my flies landing just a little further downstream. I drew them round slowly, and then I saw it – a great bulge in the water forming a large 'V' as a fish followed my flies. 'Bill! He's following.' 'Come on! Take it, take it!' I prayed silently. As I continued to draw the flies back, I was into him. The fish exploded into the air and cartwheeled magnificently before falling back and making a long first run back towards the Atlantic; it was obviously a larger fish and gave a spectacular show. It was fantastic!

It was a good ten minutes before I was able to bring the fish over Bill's waiting net. It was a beautiful, fresh, sea-liced 11-pounder and a fitting finale to a perfect night's fishing: fourteen sea-trout and two salmon in the dawn. Who could ask for more?

'Right, Bill! Now you may go to bed!' I said, and after a celebratory wee dram and photographs, we drove back to the cottage. By now it was 5 am and fully light, and the sky suggested that it was going to be yet another long, hot, dry day to shrink the rivers even further.

Bill, I later discovered, had lunch with the 'opposition'. They had been on the river for the best part of two weeks, fishing primarily for salmon through the day. Their score was nil! They were not keen sea-trout fishers and left the river for the antics of crazy night-owls like ourselves. They were a little peeved at Bill's account of our previous night's sport and our two salmon in the dawn!

This story illustrates only too well the importance of approach and tactics in extreme low-water conditions, and especially the worth of fishing in the dawn for salmon. Fish fresh off the tide, especially at night, seem to have a particularly active phase at first light, and then they go off the take completely.

Our gillie on the Helmsdale, Johnnie Sutherland, always has his rods on the water by 5 am in summer low-water conditions. They fish for a few hours until breakfast, and then leave the river in peace for the rest of the day, finding an outlet for their energy on the golf course.

On this particular day, however, I left Bill snoring gently as I headed south again, more than content. I arrived home just before 8 o'clock, in time to serve breakfast to my guests. Then it was upstairs to fall into bed and a long, deep sleep.

SEA-TROUT IN THE MIST

Having spent three weeks instructing spring fishing courses at Grantown-on-Spey I realised that not only had the sea-trout run arrived at least a month earlier than normal, but in good numbers.

I had been fishing one May morning on Kincardine Water as a guest of David Nicholson of Revack and Dorback Estates. As the snow fell gently, Norman Stone, the gillie, reflected on exciting June evenings with sea-trout which prompted David to invite me back for a few days – or, rather, nights – in June when, he assured me, I would have some terrific sport. How could I refuse?

The Spey is underrated as a sea-trout fishery, most anglers preferring to fish for salmon; but while west-coast sea-trout stocks seemed to suffer a decline in the late '80s the Spey's catches were maintained, and 1992 produced a record season for many Strathspey estates.

Kincardine Water near Boat of Garten, extends over two miles of single bank. It has some classic sea-trout pools, long and deep, with inviting tails, ideal for roving sea-trout as the light fades. The wading over gravel in the dusk is a sheer delight!

I arrived in mid-June to find the Spey at an all-time low. No rain had fallen for weeks, and the mild winter had left little snow to melt and keep the level up. However, Norman assured me that despite the conditions, stocks of sea-trout had continued to improve since my last visit and were as good as he could remember! The beat had just enjoyed a phenomenal week's sport with seventy-one sea-trout, averaging 3lb and a best of 7lb.

The bay window, Kincardine, River Spey. This was the scene of some spectacular sport and a classic sea-trout pool, with an enticingly long tail which draws slowly into a fast, gravelly run into the pool below.

With the few salmon in the pools potted and not worth the effort, Norman advised leaving the water undisturbed until evening, and we arranged to meet at the hut at 10 pm and start fishing at about 11.30 pm. Once I had tackled up, Norman took me down to the Bay Window, one of those classic pools which at times positively heave with fish. It has an enticingly long tail which draws slowly with a fast gravelly run into the pool below. It was an ideal evening for fishing, with good cloud cover and no worries about moonlight to put the fish down.

As the light started to fade, I spotted fish beginning to stir in the tail of the pool. Every now and then a quiet head-and-tail rise or the slap of a fish hitting the water raised my excitement. Having to wait was a nightmare! Although it was nearly midsummer, here in the Highlands the evenings can become quite chilly and I was pleased to be wearing Daiwa neoprene chest-waders.

I had put up my favourite 11ft 3in Bruce and Walker Century with #6 neutral density line and 6lb breaking strain leader. Norman had told me that the most popular flies were Silver Stoat variants, but David had given me one of his favourite black-and-yellow Badger patterns with a tiny flying treble. This was to prove deadly, however, this evening I decided to keep with a Lambert special Silver Stoat, size 8.

Norman told me to wade gently and work my way down slowly towards the tail, making sure that I didn't wade too far out and 'walk' on top of the fish. By now it was quite dark and the sound of fish cavorting all over the pool was astonishing, I had forgotten how exciting night fishing could be. It was easy, comfortable wading, so I started to work my way down, casting a good long line across the pool and retrieving with a slow figure-of-eight.

I had been in the water for only five minutes when my fly was pulled hard, line screamed off the reel, and my heart began to thump. Sadly, contact was short and the fish was off. Regaining my composure I started to cast again, and within minutes a good, solid pull was followed by a long run and then a fish leaping clean out of the water as it headed towards the tail of the pool at a rate of knots. After a few minutes I had the fish under control and managed to back out of the water onto a sandy beach where I could bring it ashore. Just as I had its head on the beach, with a flick of its tail, it was gone. So near, and yet so far.

Norman sent his commiserations down the pool and told me to go back into the same spot, but I fished for another half-hour without so much as an offer. Had they gone off?

June nights in the north are short and, after coming ashore for a quick dram and some reassuring words from Norman, I went back into the pool. Fishing the same fly, I waded in carefully and worked down to the tail once again. Not so many fish were showing now and I thought that I had perhaps missed the best of it. But back at the 'hot-spot' I had a tremendous pull and number three was on.

This fish spent most of its time in the air and went upstream for a change; I held on grimly and just hoped the hooks would hold. Norman came to my aid with the net and after another few minutes I had landed a beautiful fresh fish of just over 3½lb. It was my first sea-trout of the year and I was shaking with excitement. But with my watch showing 2 am, and with a busy day ahead, I decided to call it a night, leaving Norman and David to fish on.

As I drove back to Grantown-on-Spey the next evening I heard on my car radio that mist patches and a cold, chilly night with ground frost were predicted for the glens. 'Hang on!' I thought. 'This is 16 June, midsummer and all that! He must be talking about Iceland!'

Arriving back at the hut just after 10 pm, I found that already the air temperature was beginning to fall quickly under a clear sky. By 11 pm a shroud of thick mist had begun to form over the Long Pool, and the signs didn't look good. Norman suggested we went back down to the Bay Window where, despite the cold, misty conditions, fish were already indulging in acrobatics although not in such numbers as the previous night.

By now I was becoming familiar with the 'hot-spots' in the darkness, but the mist had become so thick that I couldn't see Norman fishing above me but simply heard the faint 'swish, swish' of his casting and occasional clink of his reel check. According to the books, we shouldn't have been there at all, but if it was good enough for an experienced gillie, I wasn't going to leave.

Certainly the activity and the takes were poor, but then, just as I was approaching the fast draw in to the tail of the pool, and with only a few casts left, a fish hit my fly like a rocket and the reel screamed in the darkness. I was astonished by the power that this fish showed, and my second thought was that maybe I had connected with a salmon. The fish ran hard towards the white water below and I had the devil of a job to hold him and turn him.

A fine basket of Spey sea-trout taken from Kincardine water weighing up to 5½lb. The average size was just over 3lb for Spey sea-trout. The author likes to use his Bruce and Walker Century 11ft 3in and size 6 neutral density line. Favourite flies are Silver Stoat variants and Yellow Badger, with a tiny flying treble hook. (see diagram 5)

Tonight I was using David's favourite Yellow Badger with its little flying treble, and that gave me the confidence of a decent hook hold. (See diagram 5.) The rod was bent double, and my arm was put to task, but eventually I managed to persuade the fish to change course and felt happier as it headed up into the slower deeper water above me. Norman had heard the commotion and was soon beside me with the biggest net I had ever seen. 'Ach, well, you never know, Ian!' I played the fish out and it came quietly over the waiting net. It was an absolute corker of a sea-trout, fresh and weighing just over 5½lb. A fish such as that, on a night such as this – quite extraordinary!

At 1 am I went back up to the Long Pool, where I managed to take another beautiful sea-trout of about 3lb and lost another. By 3 am Norman and I were frozen to the marrow and already the light was changing. Back at the car we found a thin layer of ice on the windscreen – the man from the Met Office had been right after all! A cup of tea and a large dram were well earned.

The next night was just as eventful, but with no frost. I took another two sea-trout of 3lb and 3½lb which again gave splendid sport. But for me catching that 5½-pounder on such a night was unforgettable.

The sun was rising as a huge orange orb as I drove back to Revack Lodge on my last morning, and roe deer grazed quietly not far from the road. While most of Scotland had been asleep over the past few nights, I had enjoyed sport such as the daytime fishers might only ever dream about.

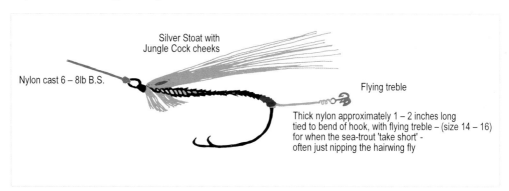

Silver Stoat with
Jungle Cock cheeks

Nylon cast 6 – 8lb B.S.

Flying treble

Thick nylon approximately 1 – 2 inches long
tied to bend of hook, with flying treble – (size 14 – 16)
for when the sea-trout 'take short' -
often just nipping the hairwing fly

Diagram 5

WAYS WITH THE WORM

Although my principal enjoyment of salmon fishing is, without doubt, with the fly rod, I have spent many a happy day working the worm. Now I say 'working' because worm fishing is indeed an art – a skill all of its own – and I think it brings out the hunter in all of us. I remember the first salmon I ever hooked and lost was on the worm. I was about fifteen years old at the time and fishing the Aberglaslyn Pass on the River Glaslyn, just below Beddgelert in North Wales. This is a popular river with the locals and you have to be up early to get a good spot after heavy rain when a roaring spate is in progress! On this day I had moved higher up above the main pools and decided to try a small run that looked promising for a running fish. I was using a rather old three-piece cane rod and one of the Allcock Bakelite reels with good heavy nylon. I ran the bait into the headstream and let it drift. Accordingly a salmon duly obliged first time down and it was on. I couldn't believe it! I lifted the rod and the fish came to the surface. We looked into each other's eyes – he turned, ran hard downstream and there was a loud 'snap' as the nylon broke. The agate in the tip ring had come loose and little did I realise it, but the nylon had been chafing and cutting on the bare metal ring. I could have cried – in fact I think I did! That was a few years ago now and hard lessons have to be learned in all aspects of fishing.

I spent many years living on the west coast of Scotland, where I owned and ran my own fishing lodge. The little spate rivers of Mull are often fast white-water pools and runs – ideally suited for the purposes of worm fishing. It was almost a question of 'self taught' as most of those estates didn't employ gillies any longer and therefore I had to learn every pool and use my own instincts and hunting ability.

There are really two principal methods of worming here, which I will describe. The first method is by using a fairly light spinning rod of, say, between 8 and 10ft in length; most of the fish tend to be grilse and summer salmon, so heavy tackle isn't really necessary. A good spinning reel – either multiplier or fixed spool – is ideal. I really like these modern reels with the rear disc drag control – it makes handling a fish much easier. I carry about three spare spools of varying breaking strain nylon – say 8–10lb and 15lb for bigger waters. At the working end of the line I attach a swivel and above the swivel I run a ball weight, which is completely free running. I attach another piece of nylon below the swivel to the hook – usually about 18in between swivel and hook (see diagram 6).

I like a fairly good sized single longshank hook which will take two to three worms completely. Now, here comes the real art and that is actually placing the worms on the hook. I tend to thread them round and along the shank, usually moving the first one or two quickly above the eye of the hook – onto the nylon – leaving the third worm complete by covering the hook and shank. An old friend of mine had an expression that the worms should be presented to the fish 'hanging like the Prince of Wales' Feathers'! Like all aspects of fishing, presentation is very important.

The worms can be purchased from a dealer, but I think it's far more fun to dig them up for yourself. I used to go and raid my neighbour's chicken run – very productive for big lob worms. The only problem was I had a devil of a job to beat the chickens – they were very partial to freshly dug lob – and quick too! I usually keep them in a metal or stone container, with plenty of Sphagnum moss. This takes

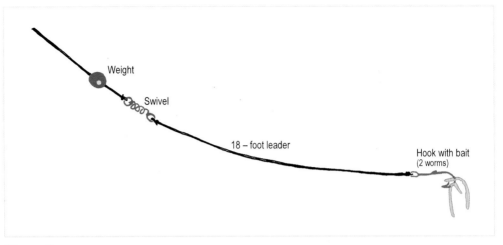

Diagram 6

away a lot of the natural slime, toughens the worms, and makes it far easier to thread them on! Damp newspaper is another good method of keeping them. Also, try to keep them cool – once the heat gets to them they deteriorate very quickly.

When it comes to fishing, you have to try to read your water and 'think fish'. It's important to try to understand where the fish could be lying if you are new to a stretch of river. Sometimes I work down from the headstream – just short casts are needed – bouncing the weight carefully on the bottom. You have to vary the weight according to water height and flow. Once you feel it is moving at the right pace without continually snagging, you've nearly cracked it. It's important to cover all the pool; try different angles, try going downstream and casting back up into the white water, gently bringing the bait back towards you. The takes are quite extraordinary. Many times it is a gentle sucking action – the rod tip will just nudge slightly – hard to believe it could be a salmon! Don't strike too soon otherwise you will miss your chance. They need plenty of time to really take the worm down. Sometimes, of

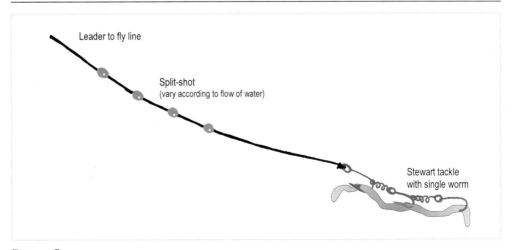

Diagram 7

course, they will take it in one go and before you know it the fish runs upstream and leaps out as the rod is nearly pulled out of your hand. It is terribly exciting – real knee-knocking stuff! Like fly-fishing, I think the actual 'take' is the most exciting part of angling.

The other method employs an ordinary single-handed fly rod with plenty of nylon and backing. The hook system is a pattern called Stewart Tackle, which comprises three smaller single hooks tied tandem to each other (see diagram 7). This method uses just one single lob worm placed on to all three hooks. The weight used above the Stewart Tackle is normally a series of split shot – again adjusted to the height and speed of water flow, etc.

The principle is exactly the same as the first technique. Often they take the worm in one go – very exciting, especially on a single-handed fly rod! Both methods are especially popular in the smaller and faster Highland streams.

CHAPTER 6

JULY
SALMON IN THE SEA...

One of the things that attracted me to living on the west coast of Scotland was the immense variety of fishing available: in the hill lochs for brown trout; lower lochs and rivers for trout, sea-trout and salmon; and, for the all-rounder, who knows what in the sea.

The west coast salmon rivers are, of course, small spate waters and not worth bothering about unless conditions are good, with plenty of rain at the right time of year. I soon discovered, however, an interesting sea loch with a tidal race running from the loch through narrows to the sea. The inlet, about 800yd long, is virtually a tidal river, ebbing and flowing, and at its head is a small spate river which at times of low water is no more than a trickle.

I arrived in mid-July and I remember walking down the loch to the tidal race and finding it alive with salmon and sea-trout splashing everywhere. It was a spectacular sight, and my curiosity was immediately aroused: would it be possible to catch a salmon in the sea?

The narrows looking out towards the sea at high tide with the tide still flooding and the scene of the author's first encounters using a copper Toby.

Local enquiries as to whether anybody ever fished there and what results they had brought only one answer:

'Och, ye'll no catch a salmon there. Everybody's tried but salmon just don't take in the sea.'

To this was added the rider that if anyone did manage to hook a fish, it would dive into the seaweed and break away. This made me even more determined to try.

I studied the water for a long time that first summer, and it became apparent that the longer we went without rain, the more salmon and sea-trout gathered in the area. In particular, the numbers increased enormously with each big tide, every two weeks. The water presented an incredible sight and we would often walk down after dinner to watch 'The Salmon Show'. Scores of silver shapes would hurl themselves into the air every few seconds. It was enough to make any angler's adrenalin flow.

First, I sought and was granted the local laird's permission to fish the north bank; it is always important to seek permission to fish from the shore within estuarial limits, especially for salmon and sea-trout. For the rest of that first summer I really only experimented, and I certainly didn't fish as often as I would have liked.

I tried fishing the fly to start with, but the seaweed and the bladderwrack snagged it on every cast; it was really frustrating, because I could see the grilse just in front of me, swimming against the ebbing tide. At low tide I could see these beautiful fish swimming amid the bladderwrack, often with their dorsal fins poking out of the water. They would turn on their sides and show great silver flashes before hurling themselves into the air. I could only assume that sea-lice were irritating them and that this was their way of trying to rid themselves of the pests.

Next I tried using a large silver Toby, which in these parts takes a lot of beating for salmon in fresh water; but try as I might, I had no success. The fish did not even look at it. All these hundreds of beautiful salmon, and they just weren't interested. Perhaps the locals were right after all!

I remember coming home one evening and looking through all my books, old and new, but I could find no mention of salmon being caught in the sea on rod and line. Most authors said simply that salmon wouldn't take in salt water. I was quite despondent. However, I tried a few more times that summer without success, but I did manage to catch a few finnock and the occasional decent sea-trout on the silver Toby, which gave me some encouragement.

Next summer I decided to have another go. It was early July and the salmon had arrived, but I didn't know then that it was the start of a long, hot spell, with no rain to speak of until September. One incredibly hot day, with the temperature well into the 80s, I said to one of my guests, 'Come on Sandy! Let's go and fling some ironmongery at those salmon. You won't catch any, but you'll see more salmon than you've ever seen in your life!'

By now, I also had permission to fish from the laird who owned the south side of the inlet. He had seen me some weeks before and told me I could have a go any time I liked from his shore. This side interested me more than the north, as it seemed to offer more potential and was not quite as weedy. Sandy and I arrived and tackled up with spinning gear. The tide was ebbing, about halfway down, and Sandy's face was a picture when those great fish started lungeing everywhere.

I decided to use a copper Toby, which I hadn't tried before, but I remembered reading about salmon being caught in the Kyle of Durness on a gold sprat. Copper didn't seem a bad substitute for gold.

We fished all morning without success, and Sandy lost so many Tobies in the weed that, in desperation, he stripped off and swam out to retrieve them. Approaching lunchtime, just as we'd decided to retreat to the pub for a bite and a beer, a salmon splashed in front of us. 'Sandy, I must just have one more go!' I cast in front of where the fish had shown and, retrieving fairly fast, so as not to snag in the weed – BANG – it took hold of the Toby. My fish fought hard, running and jumping, running and jumping . . . Luckily, the hooks held and the fish didn't go for the weed, if anything, it seemed to avoid it.

After about five minutes I was able to bring the fish over the net held by Sandy, who by this time was up to his thighs in water, trying to reach over the seaweed. That fish, smothered in long-tailed sea-lice, was fresh as fresh could be and weighed just under 5lb. It was just like catching my first salmon all over again – terrific excitement.

After a few minutes I picked up the rod and cast into the same spot. BANG! I was into number two! This fish was almost identical to the first but weighed 4oz more. After flogging away all morning, suddenly we'd had two fish in two casts; but another hour brought no more success. Once again, they didn't want to know.

I studied the fish closely during the rest of that summer. Fishing was hopeless everywhere in the long, hot spell, so I would take my guests down to this beautiful stretch of water and we would hurl our Tobies out in front of the fish. We would usually take a salmon during the course of a day, and quite often a few respectable sea-trout as a bonus.

These fish fascinated me. Their numbers increased daily, and from certain high stands, and with polarising glasses, I could watch the shoals swimming by. What I couldn't figure out was where they were heading, the tiny river at the head of the loch could not take that number of fish, there were far too many. By the end of the summer I had decided that the sea loch was a safe gathering ground for the fish, a place where they could rest after their long journey and wait for the first heavy rain to take them back to their home rivers and the spawning redds. In September my theory seemed to be proved correct as, once we had rain, several hundreds of salmon massed together – and then were gone. After that day, there was hardly a fish to be seen.

I came to know these fish so well that after a while I could identify a shoal of regulars, with one particular fish having a certain spot or mark on its head or nose or back. These marks were often net-marks or simply wounds from a predatory attack. As the tide ebbed or flooded, the fish took up stations as they do in a freshwater river. They had definite lies and they could be seen in the same places every day, side by side in shoals, quietly holding position in the tidal flow.

This was usually the best time to fish for them. If I could put a bait in front of one of the grilse that had just arrived, invariably I would hook it within the first few casts. Often a fish would follow the bait into the shore, only to return to its lie with the rest of the shoal. After such a follow I probably wouldn't hook a fish from that shoal.

The problem was keeping a fish on once it had been hooked. Being in salt water, these fish were soft in the mouth and would often throw the hook. They nearly always took to the air, and then it was a time to pray hard! Tobies can at times be notoriously bad hookers, so inevitably quite a number of fish were lost; but I managed to overcome the problem to some extent by inserting a flying treble into the split ring beside the main treble. When I caught a fish I would usually find that it was hooked by the size 12 or 14 flying treble only.

In August the success rate started to drop despite increasing numbers of fish, and the earlier arrivals, from July, started to become quite dark. Indeed, some of the later catches could be described only as black. Yet they were still smothered in sea-lice!

When some friends arrived towards the end of August, keen to have a go at these sea salmon, I told them of the difficulties and jokingly said: Why don't you throw a worm at them?' This they did and, to our amazement, found the fish very interested. Their baits, however, had to be weighted and were constantly snagging and disappearing into the seaweed. After a little thought I decided to experiment and tackled up my spinning rod with a single size 8 worm hook, three split shots just above the hook and a plastic bubble-float about 8ft above the bait. My idea was that the float would keep the bait moving over the seaweed. (See diagram 8.)

The idea worked perfectly, and by casting well upstream, we were able to keep our baits working clear of the weed. If a bait did snag, the tidal flow against the float invariably pulled it free to continue its journey. The length of leader, and the amount of lead, depended on the height and strength of the tide.

By now, I had given the various pools and lies their own names, and the lie I particularly fancied for worming I called The Pulpit. Above it was a high rockface, some 15ft above the water, on which I could stand and look down into the sea and see as many as fifteen to twenty salmon lying quietly over the bladderwrack. It was a wonderful sight, and once the fish were settled, they would usually stay on the lie until the turn of the tide.

The ideal conditions for fishing The Pulpit were under a cloudless blue sky. With Polaroids I could almost count the sea-lice on each fish's back; yet from water level they were invisible. It was under these conditions that I took a friend, another Ian, down to fish there. I positioned myself on The Pulpit and gave him instructions on where to cast, well ahead of the fish, to allow the bait to drift slowly back. We had

Diagram 8

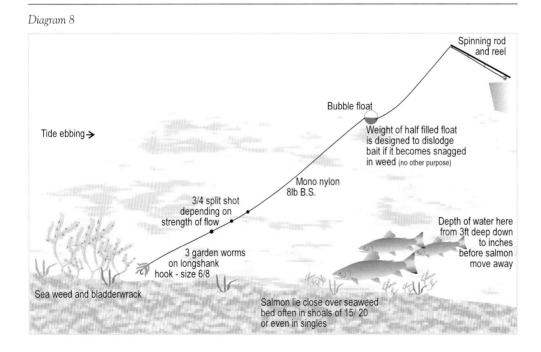

Spinning rod
and reel

Bubble float

Weight of half filled float
is designed to dislodge
bait if it becomes snagged
in weed (no other purpose)

Tide ebbing →

Mono nylon
8lb B.S.

3/4 split shot
depending on
strength of flow

Depth of water here
from 3ft deep down
to inches
before salmon
move away

3 garden worms
on longshank
hook - size 6/8

Sea weed and bladderwrack

Salmon lie close over seaweed
bed often in shoals of 15/ 20
or even in singles

'The Pulpit' looking up towards the sea loch. The salmon and grilse would lie over the seaweed shown in the picture, often with just an inch of water covering their backs before they moved off.

just enough split shot to keep the bait over the top of the weed and the float worked downstream towards Ian, keeping the bait moving at an easy pace. Every now and then it would catch the weed, but a quick flick of the rod tip soon dislodged it.

The first day only two salmon were on the lie. They were close to each other, their noses poking into the current. Ian positioned himself opposite the fish and cast well ahead of them. The bait came down towards the fish, but it was going to pass well on their outside. 'Wind in! Wind in!' I said, 'Stop! That's it! Let it run!' The bait, right on target, came down to the first fish and went virtually over its nose and back, and the fish took not the blindest bit of notice! We tried again. Still nothing! The third time the bait swung just slightly to the inner flank of the fish. Suddenly it turned, opened its mouth, and swallowed the lot. 'You've got him! You've got him, Ian!' I shouted. 'Tighten! Quick!'

He did so and was then into a real battle until, after about ten minutes, I was down beside him, ready with the net to land our first worm-caught sea salmon – just under 7lb. Our prize was one of the slightly coloured fish, but it was another 'first'. Whoever would have thought of catching salmon in the salt on a garden worm?

Once perfected, that method was deadly and brought some great catches, with a best day of four salmon on the bank and eight lost. The fish were often lip-hooked and consequently quite a few went free, but it was interesting that the capture of one salmon would not disturb the rest of a large shoal. Even when a fish ran and leapt in the air, the rest would just stay put. It was quite remarkable.

Such fishing isn't for the purist, but it gave us all enjoyable sport. Indeed, I think people standing on top of The Pulpit, watching the fish turn on the bait, had as much excitement as did the anglers.

I now had one more ambition: to catch a salmon in the sea on a fly. Despite the problem of seaweed, I had tried the fly from time to time, but the best lies were often too far out or a rockface immediately behind made long casts impossible. Added to this was the speed of the tidal flow, which from high water to the last hour of the ebb, was much too fast and took the fly off the fish too quickly.

I eventually settled on one spot as offering hope of success. The lie was at just about the narrowest part of the stretch and about an hour before low tide it was reduced to the size of a normal fly-fishing pool on a good-sized river. With no obstructions behind, it was possible to make a good cast and put out a long line.

It was about lunchtime one early August day when I suddenly had the urge to put a fly over the sea salmon. I grabbed my Bruce and Walker Century and tackled up with a slow-sink line and a size 6 General Practitioner double. It was a glorious sunny day and I reached the water at just the right time. The tide was almost at full ebb and I remember thinking that I hadn't much time before it started flooding again. Suddenly the fish showed, right in the lie, and knees knocking again, I cast my line across and put a mend into it. It looked perfect! Then as the fly swung across, the fish showed with a superb head-and-tail rise.

'My God!' I thought. 'He actually came for me!'

I cast again. Nothing. I tried several more times, but with still no response. I

The narrows at low tide. It was at this time that the author finally gained success fishing the fly on a single-handed rod and slow-sinking line.

wound in and decided to change my fly for a size 8 yellow Hairwing double. I cast across and again put a good mend into the line. It came across perfectly and then, as the fly swung round, the line tightened once or twice; but I was too hasty. I lifted the rod and pulled out of him.

'Hell!' I said to myself. 'I'm always telling my guests not to be too quick with salmon – and what do I do?'

I waited a few minutes to regain my composure and decided that another change of fly was called for. This time I went smaller again, choosing a ½-in Willie Gunn Waddington with a size 14 treble. It came over the fish beautifully. Again I felt it tighten, once, twice, three times . . . He was on!

I lifted the rod and felt the full power of the fish as he raced across the stream and jumped. My goodness! What a fight that fish gave! He was in the air at least half a dozen times after making runs which took me onto my backing. At one stage I was quite worried at having such a long belly of line over the seaweed, but eventually, after ten to twelve minutes, I was able to beach the fish on some exposed bladderwrack and then handtail him up the bank. 'What a day!' I thought, as that splendid sea-liced fish lay on the seaweed, glistening in the sun – 6½lb. At long last I had achieved my goal of catching a salmon in the sea on a fly!

A grilse of 5lb caught on a copper Toby in the narrows lies on a cover of seaweed. Note the long-tailed sea-lice attached to its underside close to the tail.

The author looking clearly delighted with his first salmon of 6½lb taken on the fly from the tidal narrows off the Isle of Mull. This stretch accounted for fish on spinner, worm and fly.

The first success enjoyed by the author in the narrows – two fresh sea-liced grilse, like two peas in a pod (5lb and 5lb 4oz) caught on an 18g copper Toby.

The invitation came out of the blue at a small social function one evening. 'I've a little bit of fishing on the estate, Ian,' the Colonel had said. 'Come and see it and tell me what you think.' Next day I duly met the Colonel on the bridge over the lowest tidal reaches of a small West Highland river.

At first I couldn't believe that anyone could possibly catch anything there, but the Colonel insisted that sea-trout were caught from time to time; however now it was low tide and obviously hopeless for fishing. The two main pools were low and gin-clear, with nothing to be seen except one or two stranded mullet. Beyond the second pool, below the bridge, the sea loch showed nothing but seaweed and bladderwrack.

I knew from previous experience that if such pools were to be productive, it would be only at the height of the flood tide and then on the ebb. Big tides occur every two weeks, and having already carefully checked my tide-table, I knew that we might well see some sport within the next few days. The Colonel urged me to come back when conditions were more favourable, and I promised to give it a go in three days' time with a friend, Peter Heddle, who I knew would be keen to try.

With high tide at 7.30 am, Peter and I decided to arrive then and fish the ebb tide, hoping to catch fish as they dropped back to the sea. Half a mile above us a small burn sent a trickle of fresh water into the pools, so the fishable area was virtually salt water, at best brackish, except when the burns came down in spate.

It was on a glorious early September morning, and the inlet of three days before was now a wide tidal river, with the flood still running. It looked 'fishy' indeed, and I felt excited as we tackled up our trout rods, mine with a slow-sink line and Peter's with an intermediate. We decided to fish two flies, a point and a dropper, and, having nothing to guide me on this water, I went for my favourite Dark Mackerel on the point and a Silver Invicta on the dropper.

It didn't bother me too much that we hadn't seen any movement as the tide started to ebb, although sea-trout often do make themselves known in such conditions. Peter said he would fish the pool below the bridge, and I went to the pool above, which was longer and wider. Some 75yd above the bridge, I suddenly heard a 'plop' behind me and turned to see rings made by what seemed to be a respectable fish. I hurriedly went on to the headstream, where the Colonel, although not a fisherman, had often seen fish showing.

I carefully waded in, and started to cast across the ebbing stream. At first rafts of seaweed gave me heart-stopping pulls, but that problem vanished as the tide gathered momentum.

Then I saw one or two fish show on the far side. I cast again and started a slow retrieve. As my flies came round, I first felt a hard pull that only a fresh sea-trout can give, and BANG! I was into my first fish. It went like a train, running and jumping all over the pool, but after several minutes I was able to put my net under a beautiful, shiny fish of just over 1lb and smothered in sea-lice. It had taken the Silver Invicta on the dropper. My goodness, how I shook with excitement! It is always rather special to try something new and be rewarded with success. Within the next ten minutes I caught two more fish of about the same size and saw several larger showing below me.

Now the tide was ebbing quickly, and I wasn't sure how long I'd have left to fish, so, after inspecting my flies and cast, I started again. Across and down went my flies and again I started a slow retrieve – sea-trout don't seem to go for a fast-moving fly. This time round I felt a pull which nearly took the rod out of my hand. I tightened hard, set the hook, and a great fish leapt clean out of the water. 'My God,' I thought, 'this is something different!'

The fish roared off downstream, hell-for-leather back to the sea. Then, with my line down to the backing, the fish leapt again and I was able to recover some line before it once more shot off downstream. I tried to gain Peter's attention, but he couldn't hear me. It was ten minutes before I managed to draw the fish close to me and put the net under it. Silver and sea-liced, it tipped the scales at 4lb 9oz, and it was another success for the Silver Invicta.

Below the bridge, Peter had seen fish and had hooked and lost one. I held up my prize. 'Come up to the top, Peter. Sport's pretty brisk!' At the spot I had vacated, his rod bent over on his first cast, and he was into not one fish, but two! It was quite a spectacle as they led him a merry dance all over the pool before I managed to get them both in the net. They were silver, fresh and just over 1lb apiece, Peter was over the moon!

With the tide still ebbing fast, I decided to go and fish below the bridge from the opposite bank. As I approached the pool, I cast and started to retrieve. *BANG!* The rod was nearly pulled out of my hand once again and I was playing another lively fish which jumped clear of the water to be followed by a second fish on the point fly! Yes, I too had hooked two at once! It was quite amazing. I had some anxious moments as one of them tried to gain the seaweed, but eventually I was able to beach one and net the other. They were two lovely fish, weighing 2lb 1oz and 1lb 2oz. This was exciting stuff!

Peter had in the meantime taken another two good fish, one a fine specimen of more than 2lb, and hooked and released four lively finnock of 8–12oz. We always make a point of releasing these future sea-trout whenever possible, though if one is badly hooked and bleeding then it is best knocked on the head.

The tide had now almost gone, the 'river' was beginning to take on its dry appearance of three days earlier, and after twenty minutes of inactivity, we decided that we would wait for the late afternoon flood. It was nearly midday anyway, and sunny and warm. It was time for a break.

As I crossed the bridge on the way back to the car, I stopped to look down into the large pool through my Polaroids, and suddenly I spotted some dark shapes in a deep hole. As the breeze eased off for a few minutes, I became aware that the hole was holding at least fifty sea-trout, lying quietly and tightly packed side-by-side, hardly moving a fin. Several of them were 3–5lb – they hadn't all dropped back by any means!

To fish for them in these conditions would have been a waste of time, but as the day progressed, it became slightly cloudier and a good stiff breeze blew up from the west, creating a good wave. We decided that a few casts might be worthwhile.

Peter waded carefully upstream of the fish and worked his way out towards two large boulders. A long cast was still needed to cover the pool, but he let his flies drift down and then made a slow figure-of-eight retrieve. A couple of fish showed some interest, but in general they were much more choosy than in the morning. Peter thought a change of fly might work and put on a longshank size 8 lure-type pattern. It worked, and he soon caught a lovely fish of 1½lb.

We rested the pool for twenty minutes or so and then took it in turns to fish. Over

Peter Heddle kneels beside a basket of fourteen sea-trout taken on our first visit to the tidal inlet. Some of the fish are actually slob trout – estuary-feeding brown trout. The best fish weighed 4lb 9oz.

the next couple of hours we caught another five fish, all 1–1½lb, with several finnock returned. We also had three slob trout, which are basically brown trout that have become estuarine feeders and do not migrate to sea feeding grounds with the sea-trout proper.

Rather than wait for the next tide, we decided that we'd had an excellent day's sport and thought it best to go home content with our basket of fifteen sea-trout. I fished the pools regularly over the next few years and came to know the water well, but I never had a better basket than on that first day and I never saw fish lying in that deep pot again.

Fresh spate water from the burn had an interesting effect. I tried fishing many times in such conditions after a high tide, but with virtually no success; as soon as fresh water came down, the fish were not interested, despite the fact that conditions looked perfect. Perhaps the fish ran the burn, only to drop back on a falling water.

The fish entered the inlet early in the season, with good catches of fish up to 2lb recorded in early April – much earlier than a run of sea-trout is normally expected in our river-and-loch systems, they usually start in mid-June.

One thing which concerned me was the danger of salt-water corrosion of my tackle, so I always thoroughly washed it in fresh water as soon as I returned home – thankfully, I never had any problems.

Sea-trout fishing is one of the most exciting facets of our sport, their quality and fighting power take a lot of beating. I've fished for them by night and dapped for them on lochs by day, but to catch them in salt water is the most exciting of all. Days spent on that little west of Scotland estuary will live in my memory for the rest of my life.

WHEN THE RIVER RUNS LOW

It was late July when I set off for a few days' fishing on the lovely little Alness in Easter Ross. I had been watching the weather forecasts for weeks, praying for the heavens to open before I drove north. They didn't however, and when I reached the Border and looked over the bridge at Coldstream, it was a shrunken Tweed which met my gaze. Further north the story was the same, the Tay, Spey and Findhorn all showing their bare bones, and not a cloud in the sky. It was going to be hard, but then I love a challenge!

I had never seen the Alness so low, despite all the efforts of Bill Topham, fisheries superintendent, to keep freshets going from the dam at Loch Morie at the top of the river. An earlier release had allowed a run of fresh fish to enter, but now he was on emergency rations. Having had trouble with poachers, he decided to open up the last gate. After that, all he could do was to pray for rain with the rest of us!

On the Monday morning I joined my fishing partner, Andrew, on Beat 2. Despite the water being so low, several pools looked promising. Bill had assured us fish were in all beats, all we had to do was to catch one! We fished every inch of water carefully, changing flies at each pool. First we dibbled the headstreams, and then put a more conventional pattern through the middles and the tails of the pools. I have never changed flies so often! But under such conditions, one must be prepared to work very hard to have any chance of success.

Having fished the lower section without moving a fish, I found Andrew upstream fishing down to the bridge; it was just before lunch and beats are changed at 1 pm. Andrew told me that he'd moved a fish to the dibble an hour earlier and had just fished through the lie again without response. I asked if I could follow him through and started to dibble the stream with my black-and-orange Hairwing tube. Nothing moved where Andrew had risen his fish, but a little further downstream I saw a lovely silver flank emerge from the depths to follow my fly all the way round, turn for it without touching, and then sink back. The fish was about 6lb and it was a glorious sight.

We saw nothing during the afternoon, so decided to make our way back for an early supper and try again just before dark. Early mornings and late evenings are often good taking times in low-water conditions, and we hoped for a sea-trout. Bill had told us that some heavy fish had run the river a week or so earlier, and Beat 2 can offer some good sea-trout fishing in one or two of its long, deep, canal-like pools, where the fish seem to hold up, never showing in the day.

We fished three streamy pools, hoping to move a grilse or a salmon, but nothing stirred. The main sea-trout pool we carefully left until after dark, when we changed to lighter single-handed rods with neutral density lines. I find these lines ideal for this sort of fishing, especially during the first few hours, when sea-trout seem more active and often show with great splashes in the tails of the pools.

I had barely put a line out when a fish grabbed at, but missed, my fly. This could be interesting, I thought. The wind was blowing strongly from the north-west by now, and it was not the usual balmy sea-trout evening. Even the clouds were building up. Was rain on its way at last?

Fish were now starting to show, one or two of them good-sized at 3–4lb. My fly was a small black-and-orange Hairwing tube with a black body and a thin silver wire rib which had brought me great success on west-coast rivers. I saw no reason why it should not work here, given a bit of luck – and it did. It wasn't long before I felt a solid thump and shortly afterwards was able to land a lovely fresh fish of 1lb 10oz. It was a great feeling, night fishing for sea-trout has a certain magical atmosphere about it.

Andrew caught and returned a couple of small brown trout and then I had another really good take. This was a much larger fish, and in typical sea-trout fashion, it jumped several times before making a couple of long runs. I had several anxious minutes before it was netted by Andrew. Again it was a lovely fresh fish, and it weighed 3lb 4oz – a good one! I had several other offers, but nothing took with such determination until Andrew hooked and landed another good fish of 1lb 4oz.

Time was marching on. It was nearly midnight. The air was cooler and the north-west wind was strengthening, so after a blank twenty minutes or so we decided to stop. We were more than pleased with our basket of three sea-trout, and our dram was, we felt, well deserved.

Next morning we were on the water bright and early, fishing Beat 5. The cloud of the previous evening had disappeared and again it was bright and warm and, despite fishing hard, we had a blank morning. Then, enjoying a cold beer and a sandwich at lunchtime beside the bridge we saw two fish heading-and-tailing in a deep hole 20yd below. The water there had little flow, and the fish were obviously holding in the deep water just above two large rocks. It seemed a likely place to try dry-fly. I tackled up with a floating line and cast and attached a suitable Yellow Dolly.

'Derek Knowles, eat your heart out!' I muttered to myself, and then went down the bank below the bridge and carefully, on bended knees, crept along the shingle bank working slowly down towards the fish. I extended line and was able, first cast, to reach the exact spot, the fly settled and looked good, and then, with a couple of quick mends, was creating a lovely wake as it worked over the fish.

Nothing! With each successive cast I was fully expecting to see a head emerging to engulf the fly, but nothing moved – not a thing.

It was at this point that a Dutch couple arrived on the bridge, where Andrew had been watching me well out of danger from my back-cast. What I didn't realise as I concentrated on the task in hand was that Mrs Dutchman had walked along the bridge to stand right behind me. I lifted, put up a good long back-cast, and . . . *thwack*!

'Oh Lord!' I thought, 'I've hooked the bridge, now of all times!' Then, as I looked round, I realised it wasn't the bridge I had hooked. The little Yellow Dolly had embedded itself in the back of the Dutchwoman's neck! Andrew's father, Colin, soon came to the rescue. 'It's all right Madam I'm a surgeon – Andrew, fetch the pliers!'

It was a most embarrassing incident and I felt awful as I stood there below the bridge, looking up as the tiny treble hook was extracted. At last it was done and the Dutch couple said a quick 'Good-bye' and were off. As it happened, that was the only 'sport' of the day. I'm still wondering if I should have entered 'One Dutchwoman' into the game-book!

Wednesday seemed hotter than ever, but as we drove up the glen road to Beat 3, the river looked a little livelier. Bill Topham had let down his emergency water to try to encourage more fish up from the estuary.

Beat 3 is in a delightful setting, and much of it runs through a rocky, wooded gorge. This can be a great advantage as much of the water remains shaded, fish are more inclined to settle and move to the fly more readily; but not this morning. We

A fine grilse of 5lb taken from the Old Bridge Pool, Beat 3, River Alness, Ross-shire – a week of incident and excitement.

fished leisurely through the welcome shade of the trees until lunchtime, revelling every now and then in wading to cool our perspiring legs!

We were both fishing long Black Goat's hairwing tubes, which were dibbled carefully over the headstreams of each pool. On such hot days, and in low water, fish seem to prefer to settle in the streamier, more oxygenated water at the heads of pools, and a well-presented dibble often moves them.

I was fishing my new 14-ft Hexagraph, Walker version, with a #10 floating line. It is a delightful rod for a river the size of the Alness and I could keep the fly at just the right angle, making sure that the dibbled hairwing created a lovely 'V' across streamy water.

I was on the Old Bridge Pool when the peace was shattered. Out of the fast, white water emerged a head which engulfed the fly in one go – BANG! He was well and truly hooked. I positioned myself on the bank and the fish came round, making several long runs followed by energetic leaps. The rod handled the situation beautifully and after four or five minutes I was able to draw the fish onto a small beach and handtail it ashore. It was a lovely fresh 5-lb grilse and first blood to my new rod.

Andrew was absolutely delighted to see my fish and told me that he had moved four fish to the dibble, but hooked none of them. He had, however, had an exciting time, and comparing notes, we decided the best of the activity had been from midday to 1 pm.

We finished the day on the upper part of the beat, which, unfortunately, unlike the lower part, was in full sun and quite hopeless. Every rock on the river bed was clearly visible, and though several pools looked promising and were, we were sure, stocked with fish, nothing moved; even fishing through the failing light of evening failed to produce any results.

Next day we were on Beat 6, but despite seeing several fish which were obviously taking advantage of the freshet from Loch Morie, we touched nothing. The only excitement for Andrew was when he moved a fish to his dibbled fly and it followed right in to the side before dropping back into the depths.

It had been a week which had looked hopeless from the outset, yet it had provided a wealth of incident and excitement.

Trying to organise a holiday at any time can be a tricky business, let alone on a self-catering family trip with complete ensemble! One August some very good friends of mine kindly offered us the use of their delightful holiday house in Aboyne close to the banks of the Aberdeenshire Dee. Now, bear in mind we have a family of three girls, one boy, a black labrador and had invited Annie's god-daughter along, so the car was already beginning to look rather loaded!

Then, of course, came the task of packing the car up with bed linen, towels, luggage, provisions, people even! 'Any chance of taking some fishing tackle?' I asked. 'Not really a lot of room left is there!' We should just be able to find room for my Bruce and Walker Century 11ft 3in just in case there is a trout loch nearby,' I said, knowing damn well there was! I managed to find some room to stow away a couple of fly boxes, and one or two reels for good measure and that was about it. I also decided to include my box of Ally's shrimps and Munro Killers as I couldn't quite rule out the possibility of a cast on the wonderful River Dee, especially if it was low water, I thought the Bruce and Walker Century would be just ideal! Finally by late Sunday afternoon we were ready to drive northwards. Travelling through the evening seems to be the best way these days and we made good time to our highland retreat, arriving at Aboyne by 1 am.

Having left the heatwave of the south I was rather surprised to see the plentiful rainfall as we approached Aberdeenshire, and of course my thoughts were now quietly turned to the prospects of fishing the Dee for maybe a sea-trout or if I was really lucky . . .! Best not to get too excited at this stage, I thought. By the time we had unloaded and got the children to bed, taken the dog for a walk (yes, she came too) and had supped my customary dram it was nearly 3 am and we were bushed.

Early the next morning I found the children excitedly exploring our new domain inside and out! I gazed out of the bedroom window and could see threatening rain clouds over the Dee valley. There were large puddles in the drive and the ground was soggy; all in all it was looking rather promising! Vanessa, my daughter, called up to say they were off to 'explore' Aboyne which usually means shopping! 'By the way,' I said, 'as you cross the bridge you will see a river gauge, just make a note of the height for me please, Vanessa as you come back.' They were gone for several hours which gave us time to gradually come to and enjoy a prolonged and peaceful breakfast! The children returned with all their news and Vanessa casually remarked, 'By the way Daddy I looked at that gauge and it reads one foot six.' I nearly choked on my coffee. 'One foot six,' I said, 'Are you sure?' 'Absolutely, we all checked the gauge.'

By now the adrenalin was really flowing. One foot six was perfect, but where oh where would I get some fishing. I made one or two phone calls to see if there was any availability but to no avail, with the fresh water had come fresh enthusiasm from fishing tenants far and wide. Indeed to see the river levels at this height in August is quite a rare sight.

Annie and I took the children off to the local swimming pool and dropped them off for an hour or two. We then both went to see our old friend Alan Brodie who has a small tackle shop in Aboyne and surely if anybody knew of available fishing it would be Alan. He had reached the magnificent age of eighty years young only a week earlier and by all accounts was still celebrating the great event! We were given a tumultuous greeting followed by a 'Come in and have a wee dram you two.' Well, how could we possibly refuse such an offer. Inside was another great old friend of ours, Ella Bowman. Ella is one of the keenest fishers I have ever met. We hadn't seen each other for years and so we had a lot to catch up on, needless to say all relative to salmon fishing! Ella said, 'Are you going to fish, Ian?' To which I replied 'Well I um . . .' 'Of course you are', she said, 'Leave it to me and I'll fix it up for you all right,' how could I refuse!

Later that evening she phoned me at the cottage to say that I could go and fish on Commonty as a guest of Stuart Spence at Invery House Hotel. Apparently he had no fishing tenants booked for that week and therefore he was delighted to let me have a day or two fishing for the house. She told me that Dan Dowell, the gillie, would be there to see me at 9 o'clock the next morning.

Next morning we were all up bright and early, Annie and *les enfants* had decided to take in the sights of Aberdeen which meant more shopping! I was given an all-round blessing and full approval to go off and enjoy a day's fishing at Commonty. Despite being offered Ella's 15-ft salmon rod etc. I decided that I would fish with my Bruce and Walker Century rod with which I have fished for salmon all over Scotland, including the River Spey.

I thought the river wasn't running that high and as I was only going to be fishing with very small summer flies I was reasonably confident that I would be able to cover

Dan Dowell, the gillie, casts his eye over Commonty Water on the Aberdeenshire Dee.

the water adequately. Luckily I was able to borrow Bob's chest waders from the cottage which I knew would be essential. I had fished once before on Commonty, only it was in February and so of course it was quite a different river now, not the mighty roar of winter flood and snow melt, but just a fine highland fly stream after heavy summer rain. I arrived at the beat just after 9 am and it looked absolutely perfect. I was greeted by Dan as a long lost friend. There were two other chaps already fishing who turned out to be a young gentlemen bridegroom and with his best man. 'They will only be here till lunch time, young laddie is getting married at 2 o'clock,' said Dan. I must admit I found it very amusing and admired the enthusiastic way in which he was spending his last morning of unmarried bliss. Dan and I both agreed that we couldn't think of a better way to pass the time on the morn of a wedding!

Dan suggested that I should go down and fish the next pool below, starting at The Bend and then work my way down into a pool known as The Loop. He suggested that I should come back up to the hut at lunchtime. The overnight rain could well bring the river up a little more and with it, hopefully, a run of grilse and summer fish. I tackled up my single-handed rod and decided to fish a size 6 sinking line, it would be essential to fish the sinking line with the smaller rod which would make sure that the fly would not be skating. With a floating line and shorter rod, it is difficult to make a big enough mend and thus stop the fly skating halfway across the river.

I could see that even at this height I was going to have to make some quite long casts and therefore it would be essential for the fly to fish from the second it hit the water. I have fished single-handed rods on the west coast for many years and because of the fast, streamy nature of these rivers have found that the sinking line is by far the best line to fish. I decided that if I did get problems of snagging the bottom I could easily change over to my neutral density line. However, the River Dee is fast and streamy and so I was fairly sure that this light line wouldn't sink too deep. I waded into the fast headstream of The Bend and began to work my way down. The water was a superb height and with just a touch of peatiness in it, but I didn't see a fish move or even have an offer until I had worked my way down into The Loop. With good long casts I was covering the water perfectly well and felt optimistic. I was able to cover the main stream and after each cast could throw in a good upstream mend. As I waded the long glide through the middle of the pool very gently, the fly was taken and suddenly I was into my first fish – what a fantastic feeling. The fish kept deep and then began to fight hard. I waded carefully back to the bank and it wasn't long before I beached a fine fresh grilse of just over 4lb. I moved back into the pool and as I approached the tail I could feel the flow of water slowing down considerably and just as I was starting to have to hand-line the fly back, the line was pulled tight, the rod bent and a respectable sea-trout broke surface and cartwheeled all over the pool. Again a super fresh fish of just over 1½lb – what a great start to the day.

Just after one o'clock I decided to go up to the hut and report my catch to Dan who was absolutely delighted to see these two fish, especially as they were the first fish to come off the beat for the best part of three weeks! I was also amazed to see that the 'wedding party' were still hard at it in the Garden Pool and said, 'Cutting it a bit fine aren't they Dan?' 'Aye,' he replied quietly. 'I wouldn't be surprised if they're back here later on, most probably just after they have cut the cake!' Anyway as it was about 1.45 pm they suddenly decided to depart and I was absolutely positive I could hear the bells ringing in the church as they drove away at high speed. The afternoon

A fresh grilse of over 4-lb and a 1½-lb sea trout started off the day with a bang! Taken on a Bruce and Walker 11ft 3-in Century, AFTM 6 sinking line and a size 10 Ally's Shrimp.

was very quiet so I called it a day at about 5 pm and thought about trying again tomorrow. After all this was a family holiday!

When I returned the next morning further rain overnight had brought the river up another inch or two and the river still looked in superb ply. Dan suggested I try down at The Bend again. It is quite amazing what an inch or two of water does to a river of this size and as I waded in this morning I could feel a much harder flow, it was also now sounding more like a large river. As I waded in I saw a fish show towards the tail of the pool and then another further downstream. This looked promising and I had a feeling that a run of summer fish was now with us, so my excitement grew. I was still able to cover the water with my single-handed rod and therefore kept my winning combination of sinking line and small Ally's shrimp, size 10, as before.

I hadn't been fishing more than five minutes and was covering the full width of the main flow, when the fly just hit the water and was taken immediately. This time it was a much heavier fish which tore off line and the little Hardy reel screamed out. After some further hectic sport I was able to carefully beach and return a coloured hen-fish of about 8 or 9lb. It was a great start and my enthusiasm was keener than ever. I didn't actually touch any more fish that morning but had seen several more and knew there were fish in the beat.

After lunch I went back to the top of the beat to fish the Garden Pool where several fish had been seen during the morning. The Garden is a fly-fisher's dream, with a fast, streamy neck running hard to the far bank and slowing into a perfect fly-fishing pace and depth. This pool fishes well right into the tail especially at this height; it is also a lot narrower here and therefore a lot easier to cover with my smaller rod. I walked well up and waded in carefully at the edge of the fast white water and put out a fairly short line to begin with. I think I had only made two casts when the fly swung back round to the edge of a large stone below me, followed by the pull of all pulls, stripping line off the reel hard and I was into number two. This fish shot off round the pool like a rocket and I had a job to follow it as I scrambled out over the large stones. The next minute it was in the air and began to tail walk all over the pool and I could see it was a really fresh fish. I played it for some ten minutes before I could feel I was winning the battle and was able to beach it and then hand-tail it out. It was a beautiful silver fish of just over 6lb still smelling of the sea! I really was going now and had enjoyed every second of that encounter.

I fished on through the afternoon with no more offers from the Garden Pool and so decided to work my way back downstream to finish the remaining hour in The Loop. With the higher water this pool fishes even better and opens up a long glide of a tail where a running fish would be happy to stop and rest. It was in this tail that I hooked my third fish of the day. Again it was a cracking little fresh grilse which gave me some terrific sport, topping the scales at just over 4lb. Three fish in a day is very satisfactory and I am normally more than content to take one let alone three. Even more

The author works his way carefully down the edge of the Loop, Commonty, Aberdeenshire Dee.

Looking down from the Bend and into the Loop, Commonty Water.

rewarding was the fact that I managed to take these fish on a river as large as the Dee with a single-handed trout rod, a light line and small fly: who could ask for more.

I arrived back at our holiday retreat at just a little past 6 pm to be greeted with congratulations and of course a well earned large dram! They were all bubbling with excitement and news of their outings around Aberdeenshire. Plans were already afoot for the next day to take in a castle or two and a trip to Ballater – more shopping! I happily agreed to join them although the thought of returning to Commonty was appealing, but this was a family holiday after all! Thank God I had packed the rod.

CHAPTER 7

AUGUST
DAYS ON THE DIBBLE

It was on the little spate rivers of Scotland's west coast that I learned the exciting art of 'dibbling' which I had practised on the Alness. These rivers rise and fall quickly, and it is essential to be on the water as quickly as possible after rain to catch them at their best.

Generally I would use a single-handed rod of 11–12ft, often my Bruce and Walker 11ft 3in Century, which comfortably throws lines of sizes 4–6. It can handle grilse and even good-sized salmon without too much trouble. Once when I was fishing for sea-trout at night, I hooked and landed a salmon on it which took me thirty minutes to bring to the net and which turned the scales at 18½lb.

For the dibble to be used to best effect, it is essential that the line is light enough to lift and skate the fly across fast, streamy water, so a long rod and a light line is the rule. In fact, dibbling is similar to fishing the bob-fly while loch fishing from a boat, where the lighter the line and the longer the rod, the easier it is to fish the bob at a greater distance.

These little spate streams can be productive on their day and are usually fairly easy to read; but they must be fished correctly, otherwise opportunities are easily missed. The rivers I have fished have been fast and gin-clear, with no long, deep holding

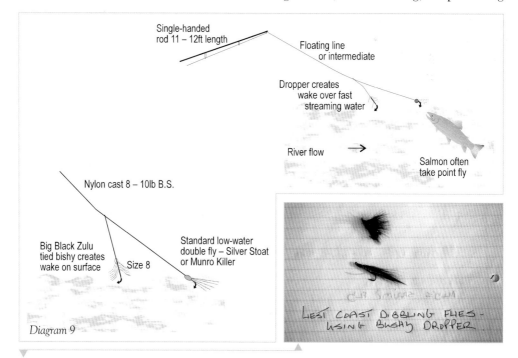

Diagram 9

Typical dibbling flies for the smaller west coast of Scotland spate rivers, using only a single-handed rod and a light line. The Black Zulu is tied on a size 8 hook with 2 or 3 black body hackles to give the extra bushy effect.

pools, just pots and runs where the occasional fish will lie. Some of these so-called pools do not fish well to the conventional across-the-stream method – they do not allow enough time for the fly to swing correctly. This is where the dibble comes into its own.

My method of fishing the dibble on the west coast rivers is different from the east-coast style, but the idea is the same, and both methods are exciting. My leader is usually 10–11ft long with a dropper about halfway down. On the point I usually have a size 10 Silver Stoat's Tail double or perhaps an Ally's Shrimp and on the dropper, a large, bushy Black Zulu tied as a size 8 or 10 single with long, black, palmered fibres to make a good wake.

Casting the fly square across the stream, I lift the rod and allow the bob-fly to skate across, making a 'V' on the surface, fishing the flies through the white water of the headstream and concentrating hard. Takes are electrifying, fish lungeing at the fly as if they are really annoyed with the skittering object. More often than not the fish will take the point-fly, but it is the bushy bob that aggravates them in the first place.

I vividly remember one demonstration of how important the dibble fly is. I was following a guest down a rocky gorge where the water roared in through a narrow opening and gradually opened into an attractive deep pool with boulders offering good resting spots for fish. I had often taken a fish from the pool and was keen for my guest, Michael, to fish it through first. By the time I arrived, Michael had just reached the tail without an offer and was changing flies.

'Did you dibble, Michael?' I enquired.

'Yes, of course!' came the reply.

I decided, however, to follow him through, just in case . . . Halfway down the pool, as I lifted the dropper making its wake across the stream and the usual 'V' in the water, up came a head, a mouth opened, and the fly was gone. Michael was getting ready to move down as I tightened into the fish.

'My God, Ian! I don't believe it! I've only just fished through that spot!' After five hectic minutes Michael netted a fish of 4½lb, shaking his head in disbelief. 'Show me this dibble method again, Ian!' he said. I went back to the same spot, put out some line, and once again I carefully lifted the dropper and watched it make its 'V' across the surface. 'See, just like that, Michael!'

As I spoke up came another head and number two was hooked, a bigger fish at 5lb exactly. I confess that old Mike was nearly on his knees! Anyway, it was a superb twenty minutes' sport which served to demonstrate that, even on a small river, it is always worth fishing over a pool again, even when you have already hooked and played a fish; perhaps the disturbance stirs the other residents into taking mood!

Another instance of the dibble's effectiveness occurred on a different small river in spate. The water was falling quickly, but running gin-clear, and I fished down a pool in conventional style. As the fly swung round near the tail, I felt just the slightest pull and a small bulge appeared in the surface. I left the pool and I went to fish upstream. After an hour, with no other touches, I returned and fished the first pool again, but this time dibbling the dropper all the way down. At the exact spot of the first brief contact a fish came from its lie like a Polaris and engulfed the Stoat's Tail on the point. I shall never forget that, it was a tremendous sight and a lovely fresh fish of 6lb was soon on the bank.

When I started to fish the Alness, on the east coast, I was soon to learn another form of dibbling which is just as deadly. The Alness, although still a spate river, is much wider than the small streams I had fished in the west, so a traditional double-handed rod of 14–15ft is needed. Early in my fishing days on the Alness I was introduced to a gentleman by the name of Arthur Chamberlain, who is a regular rod on the river and knows every stream, pool and lie. He is a master of the dibbled fly and accounts for many of his summer fish by this method.

In this part of the world the dropper is abandoned and the dibble is the point-fly. It is invariably tied on a small length of plastic tubing (¼–½in long) and usually has no body dressing at all, but just a length of black goat's hair tied in at the head. It is similar to the Collie Dog but using stiffer goat hair (see diagram). This hair is normally 3–4in long, and it is this that trails and causes the 'V' on the surface. Goat's hair has just the right qualities to dibble effectively. Bucktail seems too bulky and squirrel tail too fine.

Again, the cast is made square across the river and the rod is lifted slowly to draw the fly across the fast, streamy water so that the tube is nearly hopping. The effect seems tantalising to the fish and certainly causes a stir. I normally use a small size 10 or 12 treble, which really does hold once it penetrates.

I have seen some incredible takes to this method. I remember dibbling a Tadpole version across a mass of white water when out of the depth a huge head appeared, to be followed by a back arching over the fly and then a tail. My line tightened and I was into a salmon of between 10–12lb. Unfortunately I lost the fish a few minutes later, but the memory of that incredible take will stay with me for ever. Fished properly, the dibbled fly can add a great deal of excitement and anticipation to a day's sport on these fast, streamy waters, east or west.

A selection of Alness-type dibbling flies using a plain plastic tube with a long goat hair wing to create a wake on the surface.

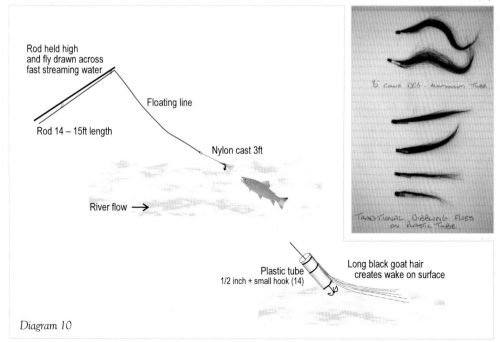

Rod held high and fly drawn across fast streaming water

Floating line

Rod 14 – 15ft length

Nylon cast 3ft

River flow →

½ COLLIE DOG - ALUMINIUM TUBE

TRADITIONAL DIBBLING FLIES ON PLASTIC TUBE

Plastic tube 1/2 inch + small hook (14)

Long black goat hair creates wake on surface

Diagram 10

Left: *Perfect dibbling water on Beat 3, River Alness, Ross-shire. On a hot summer day this angler sensibly fishes the faster streamy water which is shaded by the trees. He is using the longer rod, floating line and single tube dibble fly on the point.*

Below: *River Alness, Beat 2. Here the angler keeps well back from the water amongst the big stones and is able to carefully dibble the fast headstream without spooking the fish. The River Alness has been carefully managed and improved over recent years under the careful eye of Bill Topham. Most pools have been completely redesigned to blend in, such as the pool in this picture.*

FRENCH GIRLS, IRISH GRILSE

Annie and I came to the Erriff fresh from (weary from, perhaps) a week on the drought-stricken Alness in Easter Ross. Here, across the Irish Sea and the width of Ireland, among the Connemara hills and on the edge of the Atlantic, we surely must find water. Certainly we arrived to find low cloud and signs of fresh water in the burns, but as we drove up to Aasleagh Lodge, a glimpse of the famous Aasleagh Falls told us that the main river was still low.

The Erriff Fishery was acquired by the Central Fisheries Board in 1982, since when many improvements have been made and good management has brought increased salmon and grilse runs. It is a short river, only eight miles long, and it is divided into nine rotating beats, its headwaters are in Tawnyard Lough, a 250-acre lough noted for its good sea-trout runs.

Knowing that although it was Sunday, we could fish as soon as we liked, we got our permits from Jim Stafford, the fishery manager, and set off for Beat 3, where Michael and James, who had arrived a day earlier, were already fishing. They'd seen one or two fish, but otherwise it was the same old story: 'We need rain and plenty of it!'

Our first outing was not a long one. The fishery has simple and well-observed rules, one of which is that fishing stops at 7 pm, when rods make back to the lodge for supper. From 5–7 pm rods may abandon the fly-only rule and use worm if they wish, with a one-fish limit – but only if they haven't already caught a fish on fly. Spinning is also allowed during times of high water. The consolation for the early finish when the evenings are long is that you take over your next day's beat at 8.30 pm, so if you wish to fish after supper, you can. We were to be fishing Beat 8, an easy walk from the lodge, so after supper we thought we might as well go to have a look.

Although our evening was blank as far as fish were concerned, it had its compensations when we stumbled across a party of young French girls who, after parking their horse-drawn caravans, had decided to plunge into the river as naked as the day they were born! The temperature of the Irish evening air seemed suddenly to rise and we decided to retire gracefully for a cooling early dram and to a certain amount of hilarity from other guests in the lodge.

With a blank on Beat 8 in terms of both fish and nubile French girls, we found that we were to fish Beat 6 the following day. We had seen fresh fish moving, so despite the low water, a few were still managing to ascend the Aasleagh Falls fish pass and move up. Our hopes rose too, when Jim Stafford told us that a frontal system was moving in, with the promise of rain to come. The clouds were beginning to descend as we went to bed.

We were up and fishing by 6 am the next morning, and rain was at last in the air. Doyle's Pool, where I was fishing, was certainly active, and a run of fish had obviously moved in during the previous evening. With the water still low, I decided to fish with my ever-faithful Century and a #6 neutral-density line with a small black-and-orange hairwing tube-fly; but those fish were not to be tempted, lungeing infuriatingly across the pool and plainly keen to move upstream. They, too, had sensed the impending change in the weather and by now rain was falling steadily.

I had been fishing for about an hour when, out of the corner of my eye, I saw a fish move upstream of me, just a quiet head-and-tail. I cast quickly into the ring and the water erupted as the fish took. It really was a lively fish, 'taking off' across the pool and swimming in deep against the far bank with the reel screaming in the morning air. What a great feeling it was! Ten hectic minutes later I had the fish on its side and safely beached. It wasn't big – just 5lb – but as fresh as fresh could be, with tide-lice on its tail and head. My first Irish grilse!

As we arrived back at the lodge for breakfast, the rain started 'stair-rodding' down, and the already freshened river then rose steadily all day. This was more like it! We saw fish running through steadily, and though the water was getting rather high, it hadn't coloured too badly. I decided to stay with the fly, but I did change up to my Mackenzie Philps double-handed 15-footer. I pulled only one fish, however, at the tail of Nee's Run on a size 10 Munro Killer. Some long, deep pools on the Erriff are ideal for backing-up, especially with a good upstream wind over the deadish water and I managed to rise one fish in this way in Black Banks, but never touched it.

Next day, Wednesday, I was offered Beat 6 again, while Michael and James went off up to Beat 1 at the top. I felt no need for an early-morning start that day. It had rained hard right through the night and my fear was that the river might be too high, though it should quickly fall away. It was certainly much higher than the previous evening and looking peaty; but the general feeling as we went off to our respective beats was one of optimism. Alas, it wasn't going to be as easy as that!

At last the river started to fall, and I was continually seeing fish running through. I put up a spinning rod for the first hour or two, but had never an offer to the Toby. Then I went back to the big fly-rod and tried various patterns from large tube-flies right down to tiny doubles. By late afternoon I really had put in some mileage, but had managed to hook (and return) only two finnock. I decided to go to find Annie and have a large cup of tea.

Eventually the rain stopped and the river, falling away quickly, looked perfect. I decided my best chance might be at the top of the beat, on a long pool called Nee's Run, a super-looking stretch of fly water where I could go back to my single-handed rod. With droppers favoured on the Erriff, I chose a Black Pennell with a size 8 Ally's Shrimp on the point.

As I started in at the top, so a fish showed, head and tail, close in to the bank, almost at my feet. Alas, I was to have no repeat of the previous morning! I fished on down and was thinking how well the fly was coming across when I saw a slight bulge and he was on. The fish fought hard and made some long runs with spectacular cartwheeling leaps. It was nail-biting stuff on a single-handed rod! After fifteen minutes I was able to slip the net quietly under him – not a big fish, just 5lb and not as fresh as my first, but very, very welcome.

Despite all the rain, the run of fish had not been a particularly large one, as the counter at the fish-pass showed. No doubt the prolonged drought had seen a good many fish caught up in the miles of illegal drift-nets that operate off the Irish coast.

Next day we were on Beat 9, the lowest beat which runs into the Sea-pool below the road bridge. It is a popular beat which produced several fish during the week, but despite an early start, with the river in superb ply, I managed to move only one fish to the fly. The Sea-pool was alive with fish and they showed continuously throughout the day.

The forecast of more rain and wind turned out to be the understatement of the year! Rain set in after lunch and with it came a wind which developed, it seemed to us, into hurricane force. It was, we were told later, the tail-end of a full blown hurricane from across the Atlantic.

With the river rising quickly and fly-fishing impossible in the wind, we went back to our Tobies, and even they were blown back upstream! James eventually hooked a

James Leather fishes on good, streamy water below the Erriff Falls on Beat 9, River Erriff, Leenane, Ireland. The Erriff Fishery was acquired by the Central Fisheries Board in 1982 – good management and improvement policies have been implemented.

fish in the Sea-pool, but it hadn't been on long before it shook its head and was gone – and it was the first fish he had contacted all week! Soon after it was Michael's turn. As he stood out on a rock, rod bent, rain pouring down, and the wind blowing against him, I couldn't help but think of that wonderful scene in *Moby Dick* where Captain Ahab was struggling for survival against the elements and a slightly larger specimen! But it wasn't long before James slipped the net under a fish of about 4lb, and Michael had broken his duck.

With the river now a raging torrent, and the tide starting to flood, the little pool below the bridge looked totally different. I had seen several fish moving at the tail where the water formed a large 'V' before it fell into the Sea-pool, so putting on a 12g copper Toby, I covered the tail as carefully as I could. Tobys should really just flutter in the current, without much winding, similar to a fly, but as the bait came round, and just above the white water, it stopped as though stuck on the bottom. I lifted gently and at once I was into a fish. I managed to bring it upstream, away from the torrent below, and after about five minutes beached a shiny fresh grilse of 3lb. A number of similar small grilse had been caught during the week and we had assumed them to be characteristic of the river.

I rested the pool for a while and then tried again in the same spot. This time my Toby was grabbed hard, but after several minutes the hooks came out and the fish was gone. Within the next hour I hooked and lost another three fish in the same place. All were on for some time, and one was a much larger fish, but I couldn't hold it in the pool and it turned down into the Sea-pool and was away. I checked and double-checked my hooks, and they were all good. Although Tobys are good attractors, they can sometimes be bad hookers, probably because the free-moving hooks do not offer the best leverage.

Just before our 7 o'clock finish I saw James on the far side at the tail of the Sea-pool, where he had waded out among the rocks. I could just make out that his rod was well bent and jerking violently, so as Michael had gone for an early bath, I decided to go to the rescue. That meant running up the bank, over the bridge, down through the trees on the far bank and then wading out across the half-submerged and slippery rocks. By the time I reached him, I was completely out of breath, but the fish was not. It was putting up a lively fight, and it was all James could do to stop it running back into the sea. However, the hooks of his small Blair spoon held, and soon I was able to put my net under a lovely fresh 5-pounder, the best fish of the week.

Friday was the last day, so Annie and I decided to make another early start, and we were up on Beat 2 just before 6 am. It had rained hard all night and the river was running higher, but it was a gloriously clear morning and the signs were good. We made our way down to Deadman's Pool and I fished down with my favourite copper Toby until, just at the tail and close in to the near bank, a fish took hold. It wasn't a big fish, but it was a bar of silver, and it went straight out of the pool into the fast stream below. I held on tight and managed to coax it back and then, just as I thought I was back in control, out came the hooks. I was devastated!

Back upstream at the Quarry Pool, with breakfast time pressing, I decided to try the tail of this pool with a small Blair spoon. It was Deadman's all over again as a fish took right in the tail and the hooks pulled out almost immediately. It was time for a bath and a hearty breakfast!

After breakfast we all went up river together, deciding to fish on the far side, which meant leaving the cars at the bridge and walking up. The beat lengths are generous on the Erriff, with plenty of fishing for two rods and Beat 2 reminded me of a Highland river in many ways, as I enjoy walking as part of the sport of fishing for salmon. On returning to Deadman's Pool, I could hardly believe how much the river had dropped in so short a time, however, I left Michael and James to fish, and pressed on for the long walk up to Quarry Pool.

Jim Stafford gives all Erriff rods a map of the river showing high-water and low-water salmon lies, and for a new boy that is very useful. Still with the Toby, I started in at the head of the pool and fished down. Sure enough, exactly where the first lie was indicated, I watched a fish following my Toby almost to my feet, where it touched the bait and turned away in a great boil. Then another fish thumped the Toby a couple of times without result, and this was followed a few yards downstream by a tremendous take from a lovely fish of 4lb, not as fresh as the others, but welcome nonetheless. Although I had no other offers, that pool was full of fish from top to bottom. Later, James, fishing through the Quarry run, was to hook fish on two consecutive casts on his Blair spoon, unfortunately losing both of them and then a third in Quarry Pool just before he packed up. It was frustrating for him, but remarkable that we could have had six fish for the day.

The water fined down nicely during the afternoon and I fished my way back to the bridge with a size 8 Ally's Shrimp, but without an offer. I was, however, more than content and quite exhausted, it had been a great week. We had each managed to catch at least one fish and enjoyed much excitement and great sport – which is what it's all about.

WEST IS WHERE THE RAIN COMES FROM

Long, dry summers with cloudless skies may be wonderful for sun-worshipping holidaymakers, but they are not so wonderful for us keen fishermen. We prefer slightly more inclement weather. So when I was invited to fish a small east-coast spate river running into the Kyle of Sutherland, I was hanging on to the weather-forecasters' every word for days before, hoping to hear that heavy and persistent rain was coming in from the Atlantic to swell the river's headwaters in the western mountains. Alas, it was not to be and as Annie and I drove north, mopping the sweat from our brows, all they could talk about was sun and the chance of rain in the west by midweek.

We arrived at the lodge on Sunday afternoon shortly after our hosts, Jim and Gillian. A glance at the fishing register did nothing to dispel fears and a walk down to the gauge confirmed them. Things did not look promising. The early evening weather forecast referred to frontal systems moving into the west by Tuesday or Wednesday, but that seemed a long time away. In any case, would they reach across to the east? Time would tell.

Late that evening it seemed that the forecasters had it wrong. Heavy cloud came in and rain started to fall quite heavily. It would indeed be a stroke of good fortune if we awoke next morning to see the river in ply; but no! The morning was bright and hot again and the gauge had flickered not so much as a centimetre! I fished through the morning in shirt-sleeve order in the sweltering heat and the river was so low and clear that careful stalking was needed to avoid spooking any fish lying in the oxygenated headstreams. At lunch, having compared notes, we decided to rest the water and let the heat of the day do its damnedest. This is often the best course in such adverse conditions, waiting until early evening and fishing through into the dark. As the sun drops into the west, and the water begins to cool, then perhaps, just perhaps, you may have the chance of a fish coming to your fly. Certainly fish were moving in most pools, and we had seen one or two quite fresh fish which must have moved up in a big flood two weeks before.

Yet the persistent may still catch a fish despite the difficulties, and when we returned to the lodge for supper, there was Jimmy sitting on the back of the Range Rover with his socks rolled down and sipping a can of cold beer. He looked absolutely whacked, but lying beside him was a super little fresh grilse of about 5lb. He had taken it on a small double Shrimp Fly in the Gardener's Pool fairly late on and he was, needless to say, delighted. 'One in the house' always lifts everyone's spirits and to have a fish in the house on Monday is especially good news.

I opted for a crack-of-dawn start next morning, but as I drove up to the top of the beat, I could see we were in for another blazing day. Needless to say, I returned to the lodge for breakfast without a fish, but was lifted by the smell of bacon and eggs. Why do fishing holiday breakfasts always taste so good?

The day seemed hotter than ever and, despite the occasional sighting of a resident fish, the river was dour indeed. Yet again the weatherman was predicting rain from the west, but I was beginning to wonder if he had the right country!

By Wednesday the river had dropped by several more inches, and our chances of a fish were growing slimmer. However, as I gazed across to the west, the sky was looking decidedly darker over the mountain tops. Perhaps our man in the Met Office was right after all! Although the little river drains into the North Sea, the lodge is only some 25 miles from the west coast as the crow flies.

The River Carron, Kyle of Sutherland, Dounie. Long, dry summers and cloudless skies may be wonderful for sun worshipping holidaymakers – but are not so good for us keen fishermen.

We fished hard all day on Wednesday, and the weather was as warm and sunny as ever, but I couldn't help looking up to the western mountains, and at times they were completely covered by thick black cloud! 'It must be raining up there,' I thought.

By the end of the day my neck was curiously stiff after constantly looking over my right shoulder to the west. Many thoughts were going through my mind, but I couldn't help feeling that it was pouring with rain in those hills and that, with luck, enough rain would soak into the catchment area to give us a spate by next morning. Several times during the night I was woken by the soughing of the wind through the trees, but of rain I heard no sound.

Next morning I was again up early, and down at the river – I couldn't believe my eyes when I saw the gauge. The river had risen by a good 6–8ins, and at last was sounding and looking like a proper salmon river; but because it is a typical spate river, with no loch to act as a reservoir at the top I knew it would run off quickly. To be considered worthy a spate has to be at least 3–5ft; but after the previous few days, I was more than happy with this 8-in rise and felt far more optimistic.

We fished carefully and hard all morning, but to no avail. The sun was shining bright once more and we were again rolling up our shirt-sleeves. At noon I decided to go to see how Michael (who had joined us early in the week) was getting on in the Gorge. He had seen one or two fish which may have been running, but had no offers. The river looked superb, and I said I'd go downstream to The Field as, with a change of beat due at one o'clock, time was running out.

The Field is a lovely little pool with a fast headstream fanning out into a slow-moving but deep tail. Its one hazard is that the wading is somewhat precarious, with long, sloping and slippery slabs of rock projecting into the middle. I waded in carefully at the top and started to work my way down, covering every inch with my single-handed Century and a size 10 Ally's Shrimp. It looked perfect and I was expecting a pull at every cast.

Towards the tail of the pool the fly was coming round slowly with the current when it stopped. I thought I had snagged on a rock, but as I lifted the rod the tip went over quickly and the 'rock' began to move. I was into a fish.

Such was my surprise that I lost all concentration and, with it, my balance. I felt my feet slipping beneath me and then I was down on my backside, trying to play a fish 'bath-style'. Before I knew it, the fish seemed to sense my predicament, jumped into the air and made a spectacular run towards me. I have to say that at this point the water had poured in over the top of my chest-waders and I was thinking how wonderfully refreshing it felt in the heat of the midday sun! Michael, upstream, had seen this happening from start to finish and by the time I had stumbled to my feet he was beside me, still laughing, but with the net – and the fish did not escape! It was a bright little grilse of 4½lb – and well-deserved, I thought!

Unfortunately, the spate didn't last long, and by the next day the river had dropped back almost to its original level and the sun shone relentlessly again. Even the mountains in the west were once more cloudless.

By Saturday the cloud cover had returned, but now it seemed too late for us. As the day progressed, so the cloud became thicker and lower and steady drizzle began. By late afternoon it had turned into heavy, persistent rain. Typical, I thought, just as we had to travel home, the rain had arrived and the lucky devils fishing next week were going to get all the sport! (They did.)

In the early evening Jim and Michael announced that they had had enough and,

After a rise in water of some 6–8 inches the author caught this bright little grilse of 4½lb after a refreshing 'dip' in the water. 'Tulla' the labrador looks suitably impressed.

A fine 14-pounder on a single-handed rod gave great sport on the last evening as rain-clouds began to gather.

wet and cold, were 'to hit the tub'. I was in two minds, but Jim said, 'Go on, Ian. Have another cast down the Craigs. You never know your luck!'

So I was persuaded! Walking back down to the Craigs, feeling the heavy rain penetrating every little gap in my veteran and now tattered Barbour, I decided I must be mad. There they all were back at the lodge, in front of the fire with large drams in their hands, and here was I . . . Perish the thought! I had to change my cast which was becoming slightly on the short side after so many fly-changes and I scanned my fly-box yet again. My eye fell on one of my old favourites, a size 10 Munro Killer.

At the head of the upper pool, I reflected briefly on how many times it had been covered during the day. 'Oh, well! Here goes!' I said to myself.

My first cast landed short, I extended several more yards of line and cast again. Perfect! In just the right spot! Then, as the fly swung round in the fast headstream, I felt the lightest of plucks, followed by an almighty tug which nearly pulled my arms from their sockets. I let the fish take plenty of line and then tightened. The resistance was fantastic – I had plainly hooked a big fish on my light rod, but I felt sure it was well hooked and all I had to do was to keep my cool. The fish powered up and down the pool without showing and at one stage moved up to the headstream and then into a deep back-eddy on the far side, where half-submerged rocks showed their jagged edges.

As I tightened harder to bring him out, so I had my first glimpse of the fish. It had a tail the size of a number six shovel! 'What a fish!' I thought, and my knees turned almost to jelly.

The fish made some long runs and on several occasions nearly ran out of the pool into Lower Craigs, but each time I held on tight and managed to turn him back. This tug-of-war went on for some thirty-five minutes before I had the fish well and truly beaten. As it lay on its side, I slowly eased its head up on to the gravel and was able to bend down and hand-tail it out. It weighted just under 14lb. What a fantastic finish to the week!

My arm was nearly falling off, but I was jubilant. Back at the car I could see that the river was beginning to rise again. I laid my fish down on the bass in the car and thought of the possibilities for the next week's rods; but what the heck? Mine had been a super week. I was more than happy.

As I drove south the next morning, every river I crossed was in roaring spate. I smiled to myself and thought how lucky I had been, and perhaps next time the conditions would be good. . .

Chapter 8

SEPTEMBER
ON THE DRIFT

Until I went to live on the west coast of Scotland I had never realised how complex loch fishing for salmon and sea-trout can be. You really have to get to know your loch well and, as with river fishing, find out where the lies are. For instance, sea-trout tend to lie deeper than salmon, usually anywhere in 10–20ft of water, whereas salmon usually favour shallower water, say 5–10ft, close to the shoreline. Paradoxically, I have caught really large sea-trout in very shallow water where salmon would normally be expected to lie, usually in late afternoon or in the evening.

You also need to be prepared to fish in three different ways if the rules allow – fly, dapping and trolling – and tackling up with three different sets of equipment can be interesting, to say the least. I don't like my boat to be too cluttered with rods, so for dapping I favour one of the modern telescopic rods which can be stowed easily. It may not be the most attractive rod in the world, but it is functional and inexpensive.

On its day, dapping takes a lot of beating. Nothing is more exciting than to see a huge snout emerging from the depths as a big sea-trout engulfs your fly, and then to watch the dapping floss dip into the water as you tighten and feel the weight of the fish.

Loch Ba, Isle of Mull – a good breeze with light cloud cover and a magnificent backdrop of mountain and glen – perfect for a great day on the drift.

I particularly remember one August day when I took four guests onto our local loch. They had done little in the way of loch fishing, although the lady, Betty, had caught many salmon from rivers and was indeed a competent fly-fisher; however, dapping was to be a new experience for her.

Dapping is in fact an ideal method for people who don't normally fly-fish. It doesn't involved anything too technical, just common sense! Moreover, this was a perfect day, with a reasonable west-north-westerly breeze and plenty of cloud cover. As we motored up the loch, headed first for Shepherd's Bay and then No. 1 Bay beyond, I prayed the breeze would stay with us.

Short of our objective, Betty asked if I would give her a demonstration first, so I cut the outboard while we were still over deep water and picked up the dapping rod. I normally use about 15ft of floss, knotted every 18 inches or so, with a cast of 9lb breaking-strain nylon attached to the end, and today the wind picked up the floss perfectly and aerialised all of it from the rod-tip ring. I lowered the rod a little and the fly started to fall towards the surface.

'Now, Betty,' I said 'You must keep your rod well up, with all of the floss out . . . like so . . . and make sure you don't let the floss get wet. Then let the fly gently touch on the surface . . . like that . . . and . . .'

With that, the water erupted, a huge head appeared and the fly vanished!

I watched the floss dip into the water and struck hard to set the hooks. An epic battle had begun.

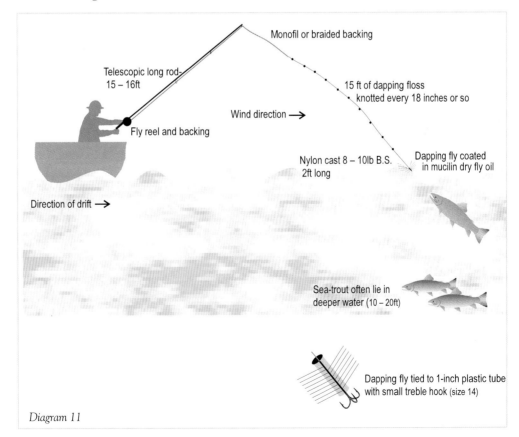

Diagram 11

A demonstration of dapping produced this specimen sea-trout of 10½lb to the authors' rod on a fine, breezy day in August.

I will never forget that first run as the fish screamed off 20yd of line, leapt into the air and followed with another long run. It really was a powerful fish, and at first I thought it was a salmon as it fought long and hard. With James on the oars, keeping us steady on course, it was a full twenty minutes before I could bring the fish to the waiting net. It was only then that I realised that it was indeed a sea-trout – and at 10½lb my best-ever! 'Well, Ian,' said Betty quietly 'That was a most impressive demonstration of dapping!'

A steady breeze is the main ingredient for successful dapping – see how the blowing floss floats well ahead of the drifting boat. This angler is fishing close to the shoreline and an outflowing burn – just the place to move a salmon in the shallower water.

When the breeze tails off is the time to abandon the dapping rod and try another method – either wet-fly or trolling.

I have discarded conventional single-hook dapping flies and always fish a tube-fly dap, usually dressed on a 1½-in fine plastic tube. My dressing is very simple: a small fluorescent-orange tag at the tail and fourteen to sixteen long-fibred red game-cock hackles tied in all the way up to the top of the tube. I match this with a small treble hook, size 12 or 14, but always a Partridge outpoint. These hooks are very strong and I have never had one straighten in a fish.

The wind eased off slightly over the next hour or so and, despite having several offers from sea-trout and finnock, we could not improve the score. Dapping can be infuriating at times, with fish coming up and splashing at the fly with no apparent intention of taking. This is especially so with salmon on this particular loch, and for them the wet-fly is usually a far more effective method.

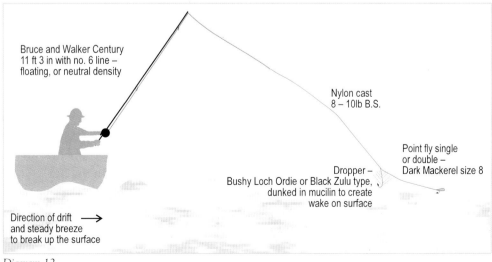

Bruce and Walker Century
11 ft 3 in with no. 6 line –
floating, or neutral density

Nylon cast
8 – 10lb B.S.

Point fly single
or double –
Dark Mackerel size 8

Dropper –
Bushy Loch Ordie or Black Zulu type,
dunked in mucilin to create
wake on surface

Direction of drift
and steady breeze
to break up the surface

Diagram 12

For loch fly-fishing I usually use a single-handed rod of between 10½ft and 12ft, and often my 11ft 3in Century. This takes a #6 line nicely and it is long enough, and the line light enough, to fish a bob-fly well out from the boat, often a large and bushy Loch Ordie dunked in Mucilin. This creates a great wake on the water and is effective with salmon and sea-trout alike. On the point I have, say, a size 8 Dark Mackerel, but with not much breeze I usually go down to size 10s and fish a conventional team of three flies, say, Dark Mackerel and Soldier Palmer with a Black Zulu on the bob.

For loch fishing for salmon, the stronger the wind the better they will come to the fly, and rough weather nearly always produces exciting sport. However, if the weather starts to blow up really strong, which it can do easily in Scotland, it is always best to play safe and head back for base as quickly as possible.

My boat is a good-sized and sturdy clinker-built 16-footer which takes two rods comfortably, with myself on the oars. I like to have the dapper fishing on my left and the wet-fly fisher at the other end of the boat, out of the way of hazards of wandering floss line! However, with a left-handed wet-fly fisher, I reverse the order. Sometimes the wet-fly won't interest the fish and the dapper does well; sometimes it is the other way round, with the wet-fly getting all the sport and nothing showing to the dap.

A bank-fisher will often do surprisingly well by working slowly along the margins of a loch, especially when a good breeze is blowing along the shoreline. I remember once when we went ashore because one of my guests wanted to change his cast and I walked only a few feet from the boat, put out a line and hooked a salmon on a Black Zulu virtually at my feet. The hook did pull out and gave the fish its freedom, but the incident demonstrated a point.

On the day of which I write, having spent the morning fly-fishing and dapping over the salmon and sea-trout drifts, I decided that it might be worth trolling on the way back to see if another guest, Michael, who had been bank fishing, could pick up a salmon. Trolling can be a most effective method, with usually a Toby fished 35–50yd astern on each side of the boat. It's a good method to employ on the way back to base, in the knowledge that the water will be well rested afterwards.

I have also caught salmon on a team of flies trolled behind the boat, and often, if the

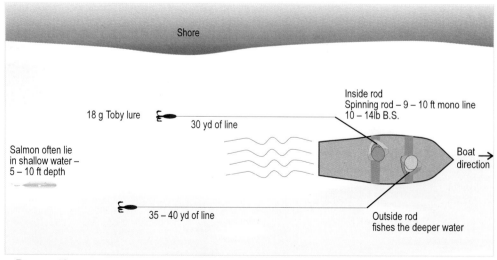

Diagram 13

wind dies, making dapping hopeless, it is worth trying what I call a 'row-troll'. Instead of using the outboard, I simply row the boat over the lies with two fly-rods trolling with sinking lines. The method causes little disturbance and can be very effective – not least in taking off those extra pounds put on by good breakfasts and dinners!

I never cease to be amazed that you can troll shallow water from an outboard-powered boat, watching the rocks below, yet still catch salmon. The noise and disturbance doesn't seem to bother them as much as it does the sea-trout.

On this particular loch I prefer an 18g silver Toby, although I have had success with other colours and with Rapala lures, it really is a question of having confidence and fishing with the lure which catches most consistently.

On the big lochs, such as Tay, Ness and Lomond, where trolling is big business and three rods are often used, rods are set into rod-rests and the anglers wait for the fish to take. However, I like to hold the rod because, for me, the actual take is the most exciting part of any fishing. I love to feel the initial contact which sets the adrenalin flowing. The fight is always fun, but that first take, whether to fly, spinner or worm is a magical moment not to be missed. With trolling it is sometimes just BANG! as the lure is taken in one almighty gulp, the rod bends and the fish jumps before racing off; at other times a fish will give the bait a couple of thumps before the final take, and that, too, is exciting. But it is always vital to make sure that the tension on the spool is set light enough for the fish to take line in the initial rush, but tight enough to set the hooks.

On the day I have mentioned, as the baits were set slowly further behind the stern, I put the boat on course to keep close to the shoreline and to fish over every possible lie. I always fish the outside bait furthest astern, so that it fishes a little deeper, but, by and large, most fish seem to go for the bait nearest the shoreline.

We had motored for only about 200yd when, as we went round a bay, Michael's rod, on the shore side, went over a couple of times and he was into a lovely fresh fish which showed straight away. The other line was quickly reeled in and I took the boat gently offshore with the salmon following obligingly. Once in deeper water, I cut the outboard and got on the oars, this is when the fun and games often begin. A salmon usually tries to make for its shallow-water lie with long hard runs. Then it will try deep-water tactics, often boring down and following with that agonising head-shaking! Today, after about ten minutes, the fish was on its side and Michael drew it over the waiting net – a lovely fish of 6lb.

As we drew in for lunch, I reflected that we had had a superb morning's sport, and prospects for the afternoon looked good, provided we didn't lose the breeze. We were in luck, for the wind picked up again, and we hadn't been drifting long when Michael's father, 'Skipper', who had now joined us, had an offer to the dap and was playing another hard-fighting sea-trout which gave tremendous sport, its long runs followed by spectacular leaps that only sea-trout can perform. It took Skipper fifteen minutes to bring it to the net, and it weighed in at a respectable 3lb 12oz.

Later on it was the turn of young James, who caught a fresh fish of 1lb 2oz. Indeed, sport was good all afternoon, with three finnock caught and some really large sea-trout coming to the dap, but never taking hold; however it was great fun and exciting just to see the fish boiling at the fly. Dapping demands 100% concentration and can be quite mesmerising as you watch the big, bumbling dry-fly moving from side to side over the waves. Given the right conditions, such as that day in August, loch fishing for sea-trout takes a lot of beating, and I for one won't forget the day I caught a 'demonstration fish' that turned out to be the sea-trout of a lifetime!

ENCHANTED EACHAIG

I had often heard stories of the huge sea-trout runs which take place on Argyll's delightful little River Eachaig on the west coast, but I had only dreamed of fishing the river until a friend who had bought a time-share on it asked me to join him for a few days. It was to be a rewarding experience.

The river flows from Loch Eck and runs for about 4½ miles through a beautiful wooded landscape down to the sea at Holy Loch. It has forty-five named pools with deep holding water and smaller pots and faster-flowing water in rocky gorges. It also has some lovely long, sweeping pools that offer first-class fly-fishing.

The fishing rights on the whole of the river were bought in 1984 by Salar Properties; their first priority was to remove the nets from the estuary and Loch Eck. Some massive catches of sea-trout have been taken by these nets in past years, for instance, in 1977 one sweep of a net took 510 fish! The largest net-caught sea-trout was one of 28lb taken in 1974, and fish of up to 15lb have been taken frequently.

The rod fishing was just as impressive. In 1978 one rod caught twenty sea-trout weighing a total of 62lb in one day. On another day in the same year five sea-trout were caught weighing a total of 51lb, the biggest 14lb! The removal of the nets has improved the rod-fishing dramatically, in particular, the salmon and grilse returns have shown a significant increase.

The fishing is divided between three beats, with four, three and three rods per beat, which are fished on a downward rotation, changing at 3 pm and, unusually at 3 am. This is for the benefit of night sea-trout fishers during the early summer months, but towards the back-end the mid-afternoon change has the disadvantage of giving a long morning session and a short afternoon session. However, Bobby Teasdale, the full-time bailiff, has had more than ten years' experience on the river and knows it intimately.

As I set off for the Eachaig in early September, I was full of anticipation and hope, especially as the rain fell more heavily as I drove westwards. It was still pouring down when I arrived on the middle beat just after lunch on the Tuesday, yet the river was running gin-clear and looked in superb ply. It seemed ideal for my usual Century with a slow-sinking line and a 1-in black-and-orange Tadpole-style tube-fly.

My host, George, and his son, Lee, were fishing downstream; they had caught two salmon the day before but nothing today. However, George was optimistic, and with an hour to go before the change-over, I was instructed to fish the Hut Pool and then down to Fail-me-Never.

The Hut Pool is a wonderful stretch of fly water and looked in superb order. I started off at the gauge and worked my way slowly down the pool, putting my fly across to the far side with a good upstream mend. I had been fishing for only a couple of minutes, when I saw a movement to the fly and, *BANG*, a lovely fresh salmon jumped clear of the water and tore off line. Salmon give tremendous sport on a single-handed rod, and it was a hectic ten minutes before I had the fish on its side and then on the beach. The Eachaig has super, gravelly beaches which make landing a fish easy. George and Lee were delighted to see my fish when I walked back to the car.

The rain still fell relentlessly as we moved down to the lower beat, but George had only just started fishing the head of the Barrel when he rose and hooked another lively fish of 7lb on a Shrimp Fly. I managed to hook two rainbow trout of about 1lb apiece, escapees from a fish-farm along the coast and just two of many of these fish throughout the river. Escaped rainbows seem fairly common on many west-coast

A lovely sea-liced 7½-pounder – the freshest of the week taken in Lamonts by George Pilkington.

rivers, which I find slightly worrying. Rainbows are voracious feeders and must do immense damage to salmon and sea-trout parr, as well as bringing the risk of disease, we must hope that something can be done to stop such occurrences.

Next day we were on the top and middle beats, rain had poured down all night and the river was high, but still gin-clear. Our best bet seemed to be on the Still Pool, a slow-moving, canal-like pool on a long bend. It looked perfect, and Lee, fishing a floating line, rose two salmon which didn't connect. I had now set up my double-handed rod for this large pool, which I thought I would fish by backing-up. I cast fairly square across and moved two or three paces upstream and made a slow hand retrieve. Takes to a backed-up fly can be electrifying, but today I had only one offer to a small black-and-orange tube-fly.

Down on the middle beat, I was sent on to fish the superb Ballachyle Pool, a lovely looking stretch of water which can take a good hour to fish properly, especially at the prevailing height of water. I fished carefully all the way down, but it wasn't until I reached the very tail of the pool that my tube-fly was seized with a deep, vicious take. With George's help I eventually netted a fine 7½-pounder.

Moving down to the Hut Pool, I asked George if I could fish it through. 'Go on, Ian. We've fished it three times, so you might as well have a go,' he said. By now it was nearly 7 pm; the midges were starting to be troublesome and I was just thinking that I couldn't bear them any more when, near the tail of the pool, and over a likely-looking lie, my fly was grabbed and yards of line screamed off the reel. Taken unawares, despite the good-looking lie, I nearly fell in with shock, but managed to tighten on. It was a strong fish, and when I eventually managed to beach it further up the pool, it turned the scales at a respectable 9lb 2oz.

We awoke next day to find the skies opening up yet again and the river starting to rise once more. I moved a couple of fish in the Barrel, but they just rolled over the fly without touching it. Upstream I found George fishing Lamonts on the far side, and was just in time to see him tighten into another fish. The freshest fish of the week, it was a lovely sea-liced 7½-pounder which took a 2-in ivy-gold Waddington on a sink-tip line. Up on the top beat, after change-over, I decided to give Steam Boat Pool a go; it had been far too high the day before, but was now coming into good ply. I'd been in the water for only a few minutes when, as the fly came down in the headstream, I was taken by another fish of 7lb. This was the only fish of the week that didn't put up a good fight.

On Friday we were back on the middle beat, the rain had eased off and the river looked perfect. I pulled a fish in Wood Pool early on, but that was all. I had, however, noticed a promising stretch of water just above Wood Pool, though it wasn't on the map as a recognised pool. Finding a place upstream to wade across, I worked my way down to this 'unknown' pool. It looked ideal, and the fact that branches had been cut on the far side made it very fishable. 'I must have a chance here!' I thought.

I worked carefully down and about halfway hooked a sea-trout of about 1lb – our only sea-trout of the week. Then, down towards the tail, I had a small pull. It could have been a parr, but I had a feeling it wasn't and as I went back up to the headstream, a salmon showed.

Changing down to my 1-in black-and-red tube, I fished through once more, and at

Two fish from the 'unknown' pool on the River Eachaig. A 1lb sea-trout and a 5lb grilse, which came to the fly three times before being hooked.

exactly the same spot I felt another tiny pull which had to be a fish! So I changed flies for the third time and put on one of my real old favourites, a size 10 double Silver Stoat's Tail.

Going back up to the head of the pool, I worked my way down again, and, as I approached the lie again, I cast across and my fly was taken hard – a grilse of 5lb. It had been an exciting morning. Bobby Teasdale was delighted when I told him, especially as he had cut the branches only the day before, feeling sure that it was going to be a promising pool.

Our last day saw young Lee take a fish of 7lb 4oz from the tail of Wood Pool just before dark to a Shrimp Fly. He was delighted, as he hadn't touched a fish since Monday morning.

We ended the week with ten fish, which for a small west-coast spate river was an excellent result. I was surprised not to see many sea-trout, but they do tend to run in June and July through to August, and they don't waste any time in getting to the loch. In any event, for me it had been a week of enchantment on a superb little west-coast spate river.

Although I had fished on many of Scotland's west-coast rivers, Ayrshire was one county I had never visited until a friend invited me to fish on the Doon, where he had bought a time-share on the Smithston Water, near Dalrymple. I've always enjoyed fishing the smaller salmon rivers and my first sighting of the Doon after a long drive made the adrenalin flow. It was typical of the type of water I like to fish, inducing feelings of both challenge and expectation.

The Smithston and Carnachan time-share beats together make up about 2½ miles of fishing, of which 1¾ miles are double bank, with twenty-one named pools. Old pools have been improved and new pools created on the middle and lower stretches, and a fishing cabin – more like a lodge than a hut – has been built in a particularly attractive location. Some of the new pools have already proved productive.

The Doon follows a westerly course from its headwater in Loch Doon and flows through beautifully wooded country for some 23 miles to the tide at Ayr. The river is fortunate in that it enjoys a good flow of water, supported by the resources of Loch Doon and regulated at the hydro-electric dam, so that even in times of low summer rainfall, the river has a daily compensation flow, especially from July to October, the principal fishing months. Great improvements have been made since the Doon Angling Improvement Association was formed several years ago. The association works closely with the District Fishery Board in the control of poaching and pollution and in hatchery and stock improvement. A team of vigilant and hard-working bailiffs keeps watch on the river, and a hatchery produces fry from native stock which are planted into the river each spring.

It is hoped that the estuarial netting station will be bought-off and then Doon will surely be one of the great salmon rivers of Scotland. In 1988, more than 1,800 salmon were caught, an outstanding return from such a small river.

Smithston's resident gillie, Colin Mackenzie, is an amiable and cheerful young man and as keen as mustard; but he could do nothing about the water level, which, despite previous hopes of heavy rain had lifted only about an inch. Bearing in mind the long, dry spell, that wasn't altogether surprising, the ground was hard and would take a lot of rain before letting it go to lift the river and bring up a run of fish from the estuary. Little did I realise what was coming in from the Atlantic – the remnants of a westerly Atlantic hurricane!

Today, however, was clear and bright, and altogether pleasant. Colin put me on the top beat, with a change to the middle and lower beats after lunch. I quickly tackled up my usual Century with a #6 neutral-density line and a size 10 Ally's Shrimp on 8lb b/s nylon. I love to fish a small river with a single-handed rod, especially in the conditions which prevailed. The water was gin-clear and I fished carefully through each pool. The fly fished well, and my anticipation was high, but despite signs of the occasional resident fish, nothing was prepared to take a close look at my offering. My fishing partner on the beat was Stella, who had been fishing the middle beat and had risen a fish twice on a small Shrimp Fly, but, alas, had failed to connect. After lunch, on the middle and lower beats, Colin took Stella down and I followed on the opposite bank.

A new stretch of water is always a challenge as you try to read each pool and run as you approach. Where will the fish be lying? Where will one take? Are any fish in the pool in the first place? All these questions went through my mind, but they are all part of the pursuit of salmon. I have always had a hunting instinct, and I love to explore every nook and cranny in a pool, searching behind every rock in the hope of feeling that heart-stopping pull from a salmon.

Having had no success with Ally's Shrimp, I changed to another old favourite, a size 10 Munro Killer. The water on the lower beats tends to be faster and streamier than higher up, with many pots and runs. In fact, the topography of this lower beat reminded me of a typical west-coast spate river.

I pulled a fish in a small pool called Scoot Hole, and then, as I worked my way downstream, found the river divided in two by a large, wooded island. A fast stream ran down my side, broken here and there by large boulders – not exactly what one might call a pool, but just the place for a fish to stop off for a breather. The fly doesn't have long to fish in this type of water and it is essential to try to hang it in every likely-looking lie. One large rock on the far side had a super little lie running off it. It looked promising and my cast was accurate, the little fly plopping in just below the rock. Within seconds it was grabbed viciously and my reel screamed as the fish took to the air – it was a fantastic take.

It was now that my problems began, for this was fast, heavy water with little room in which to play the fish. I held on hard as it tried to dash downstream before throwing itself into the air again. It was a lovely, shiny-bright fish, and I prayed that the hooks were fast. It was at this point that Colin, who had seen me from the far bank, crossed the river like a roebuck to come to my assistance. I was delighted to see him, as I wasn't at all sure where I was going to land this fish.

McKenzie's Pool, River Doon, Ayrshire.
Having started the week fishing a single-handed rod and small flies, the rain set in hard, bringing the river into a roaring flood and a change to 15-footers and large flies was called for.

It was still using all its strength in the fast, white water to try to gain its freedom. However, within a few minutes, I had the fish close in and Colin was able to net it – a 'cracker' of just under 7lb, and a lovely shiny-fresh fish, too, not long from the sea.

It was a good start to the week, but somewhere along the bank I had dropped my aluminium fly-box containing all my favourite Ally's and Munroes. So on the one hand, while feeling elated with my prize, I felt rather low about losing some good old friends. I searched the banks carefully, but never saw the box again.

By now the sky had changed colour and the weather was looking threatening. The TV weather forecast that evening made it clear that we were in for a rough ride, the hurricane was about to pay us a visit, and as I dropped asleep I could hear heavy rain beating on my bedroom window.

Next morning the river had risen by 8 or 9 inches and was flowing the colour of coffee! My cousin, Peter, had arrived to join me for the rest of the week, and, despite the height and dirty water, we did make an effort to fish; but it was hopeless.

During the afternoon the rain set in again, persisting overnight. By next morning the river was back to its original height, although the colour had cleared slightly. We fished hard all day, using our 15-footers and large black-and-yellow tube-flies, but we never saw a fish – obviously the water was still far too high. The encouraging aspect lay in the reports of a number of fish being seen below us, running up from the sea. If the river fell and settled, we might be in with a chance.

The river looked much better next day, having dropped several inches and, more importantly, the colour showed a great improvement. The weather had turned a bit cooler and was still blustery and again we decided to use our big double-handed rods with slow-sink lines, with my choice of fly a black-and-orange aluminium tube. We were back on the top beat, and I felt far more optimistic. I had seen the weather forecast, however, and knew that time was against us yet again!

I saw a fish in the Whisky Hole, pulled one in Seggans', and saw a couple of other fish below me, which was promising; but after an hour I decided to go back up to the Whisky Hole and cover the fish I had seen earlier, changing down to a size 8 double Shrimp Fly on the advice of my friend Carlos van Heddegem, a first-class fisherman who has spent many years on the Doon and always insists on small flies and single-handed rods right up to the last day of the season.

The Whisky Hole looked so good that I expected a pull at every cast as I worked my way down. Close to the tail, on the far side, lies a large rock with a superb stream coming off it, which was where I had seen a fish show earlier on. I covered every inch and as the fly came back onto my bank and I started to lift the rod while slowly hand-retrieving, suddenly the rod was nearly pulled from my hand as a fish took hold.

Now, because I had hooked the fish on the dangle, I knew that he probably wasn't well-hooked. Peter, fishing upstream, had seen that I was into a fish and came down to lend encouragement. By now the fish had been on for five to six minutes, but he had made no spectacular runs, indulging only in a lot of head-shaking and rolling, which I hate. Peter extended the Gye net and then the fish, which was on its side, made one more roll and came unstuck! I'm sure that fish was hooked only lightly on the snout and it was only a question of time before we parted company, but he had given us a bit of excitement – and renewed our enthusiasm.

Unfortunately, by lunchtime the rain was descending once more, and by mid-afternoon the river had risen to new heights and was back to its old coffee colour.

Friday brought another massive flood, although the water had cleared considerably.

We both fished hard all day, but saw only one fish, in the Whisky Hole, during the evening. Reports were still coming in of a number of fish seen and caught below Dalrymple, and it seemed that the fast, heavy white water between Smithston and Dalrymple must be holding them back. If only the level would drop, then we and higher beats might be in with a chance.

The Gods were with us, for that night it didn't rain, and by Saturday morning the river was running down to the best height we had seen all week. It still seemed high on the lower beat, but after lunch, back on the top beat, we were faced with a river that was in superb ply and running gin-clear.

Now I was back to my single-handed rod and my small double Shrimp Fly. I was on Polnessan when I spotted the first fish running through, or so I thought; perhaps they really were on the way! Then, fishing down on Thorn Tree Pool, I pulled a fish but he didn't come again. Another five yards or so downstream, the fly stopped on the far side of the run and line slipped through my fingers, followed by a long *WHIRR* from the reel. I lifted the rod, tightened, and yes, this one felt much better and I was sure the hooks were well in. That fish led me a merry dance and was so strong that I couldn't seem to tire it. It made some spectacularly long runs up and down the pool, sometimes throwing itself out of the water, so I could see it was a good fish and quite

Thorn Tree Pool, River Doon. By Saturday the water had fallen back to enable the author to fish his single-handed rod and he caught a fine fresh cock fish of 10lb.

fresh. Eventually, after twenty-five minutes, I had it on its side and was just about to hand-tail it in a difficult situation when I heard Colin shout from behind me. 'Hang on! Hang on, Ian! I'm coming with the net!' To say that I was delighted to see him is to understate the case! He gently put the net under my fish and lifted it on to the bank – a cock fish weighing just over 10lb. My right arm felt as if it was going to drop off. What a superb fight it had been!

Several other fish had been seen and pulled further upstream, Colin told me, so it seemed that a good run of fish had come; but by now it was 5 pm and the week was drawing to a close. Just before seven o'clock I pulled another fish twice, but it didn't come again, despite a change of fly. Such short-taking is often the behaviour of running fish, intent on moving on. It had been a challenging and rewarding week and an absolute delight to fish on such a wonderful fly water.

This story has a sequel. Two weeks after I returned home I received a phone call one evening from Head Bailiff, Carlos, who told me that my fly-box had been recovered by a local angler, Jock Barclay, fishing 6 miles downstream from where I had lost it, just above the tidal reaches! I was bowled over to think that the box and flies, somewhat muddy, but intact, had been handed in. In this day and age it is encouraging that somebody should take the time and trouble to try to return a box of flies. One's faith in human nature is restored – thank you, Mr Barclay!

COME HELL AND HIGH WATER

Autumn on the Banffshire Avon (A'an) had already proved exciting and productive for me and my guests and we had also witnessed every aspect of our September weather systems, sometimes all at once! However, when we reached the top beat on the Friday morning we hadn't fully appreciated how much rain had been falling through the night. Our first glimpse was a very swollen and peat-stained River Livet which is a main spawning tributary of the Avon. This river is normally quite easily wadeable but now a torrent of water was pouring through Glen Livet and into the River Avon.

The Avon had risen by a good 12 inches and still stair rods descended from the heavens. We surveyed the Livet mouth and then went down to have a chat with my friend Bill Appleton who was fishing a little way downstream. We placed a marker stick at the edge of the river and walked down to see Bill. We advised him that today was definitely a day for large brightly coloured flies such as a 2-in Waddington and just let it fish through the main stream and dangle it down along the edges. The main bulk of water was far too big to be holding any fish, but of course there is always a chance of picking up a running fish in these conditions by dangling the fly close in at the bank. Indeed, as we spoke to Bill, a good fish showed a little way downstream,

Dalmenach pool, River Avon (A'an), Ballindalloch beat, Banffshire.

tucked in by the bank and probably running like fury! After spending about half an hour with Bill we walked back upstream and returned to our marker, and we were quite surprised to see that the river was already starting to fall by an inch or two, and at least the rain had begun to ease. Michael and I had booked the upper part of the river, which to date we had not been able to fully investigate with the fly-rod, and we were, therefore, keen to get a move on, especially as this beat covers some 2½ miles of quite remote and wooded walking. Vehicular access is difficult and so it's a case of walking upstream and travelling light. This type of fishing is always exciting and I love exploring new water, finding new pools, glides and runs which often are not even marked on any of the beat maps; to me this is the essence of fishing – it's what I call 'hunting fishing': 'hunting fishing' is really a case of exploring new water and being able to read the water, find the lies, and hopefully find a fish along the way!

Despite the high water conditions we both opted for our smaller and lighter rods, no need for 15-footers here! I took my 11ft 3in Century and Michael fished his 12ft 6in Walker. We crossed over the suspension bridge and walked up through the trees for several hundred yards until we came to an opening just below one of the main pools. Indeed, that pool looked very promising, but totally overgrown from our side, and virtually impossible to cover with the fly. However, there was a superb-looking run below which we had spied at earlier in the week on a brief recce of this beat. The water had been far lower then, and we had seen fish showing in this run on the far side, right under the overhanging trees, which was where the main stream of water was flowing. Now we were faced with a roaring torrent pushing through the middle of the river and the usual lies would not be occupied. However, from the middle stream to our bank looked absolutely perfect and the chances of finding a resting fish seemed promising. Fishing a 1-in aluminium black-and-orange Aros tube-fly I made a few casts at the headstream and the fly fished perfectly in to our bank. I was beginning to feel confident and the black-and-orange tube looked good in the peaty water. I had only been fishing for a few minutes and, as the fly came round in to the dangle, suddenly the line tightened and the reel screamed quickly and briefly; no sooner was he on than he was off. I couldn't believe it, and neither could Michael. This, of course, is often the problem when fishing in these conditions – if you take fish on the dangle they are often hooked just in the snout of the nose and I suspect this was a typical dangle-take, hooked in the snout – on and off; however, it had already proved a point! Just then we spotted a fish head and tail, just by a wee bush, not even a foot from our bank and about 20ft below us. Here was a fish lying in water that would normally be just a gravel bank and we would normally be fishing from that bank. I covered him several times but to no avail. I carried on fishing down and kept as close to our bank as possible, however, it was becoming difficult because of a number of overhanging trees and it soon became necessary to get in at the edge and wade, keeping as shallow as possible. I had seen a large rock below me which I felt could possibly be holding a fish close to it, and just as the fly swung above the stone I had another solid pull. I covered the lie again and this time the fish came to me a second time, another good solid pull, but it did not connect. It was incredibly frustrating, but also very exciting and by now my adrenalin was beginning to flow, I fished right on down to the fast white water without any further offers.

Michael and I decided it was time for lunch and sat down for some hot soup, followed by a large dram. At least the rain had stopped and having got soaked on the outside we decided it wouldn't do any harm to be wet on the inside! Although we still had plenty of water to go at further upstream we had become quite obsessed with this streamy glide and after resting it for an hour or so decided to give it another cast. Michael went ahead of me this time and I followed him down. I actually pulled a fish just by the little bush where we had seen that fish head and tail earlier, but it was just a brief pull, and didn't come to anything. Yet again I imagined this was most probably another running fish, often a running fish will stop briefly and will just make a tentative snatch at the fly, not really intending to take it.

Michael by now was well downstream negotiating those overhanging trees when I suddenly heard him call out 'Ian, I'm into a fish.' 'Bloody typical' I thought as I made my way down through the thick undergrowth to go to his aid. By the time I got to him, Michael was looking quite grim-faced, trying desperately to keep the fish under control, and at the same time, keeping his rod-tip away from the overhanging branches. In this fast stream there was nowhere to beach a fish, and without a landing net it was not going to be easy. This was certainly one hell of a place to hook and land a fish! I carefully scrambled in off the steep bank and down beside him and he had to play the fish right out; then, when it was ready and close to the high, grassy bank, I was able to hand-tail it out and lift it up on to the bank all in one go. It was a super little fresh cock fish of just over 6lb and by now Michael was grinning from ear to ear.

After the usual customary celebrations, with a large dram, Michael decided that he would go back to the head of the pool and let me fish through to the tail. The whole of this tail looked very promising despite the tricky overhangs. Simple, short, single Spey casts were all that were needed before letting the fly swing in onto the dangle. These fish were, without doubt, right under our feet! I fished on down very carefully and as I approached the tail of the glide just before the fast white water, I spotted another large stone which was covered and creating an enticing large 'V' in the water – it looked very promising. Indeed, just above that stone, and as the fly swung round it was taken hard and my reel screamed out. I lifted the rod and felt the full weight of the fish as it turned and started to run downstream fast! Michael had heard my reel scream, and was soon making his way down towards me. I tried to turn the fish, but by now it already had its nose into the white water and was heading back towards Spey bay. It was a tug of war between us and I knew it was going to be a losing battle. Sure enough the hooks pulled out and another fish was gone – I couldn't believe it. By the time Michael reached me I was sitting on the bank, head down and inspecting my hooks. Michael also couldn't believe my bad luck as we sat and looked down at the fast white water where the fish had managed to make its escape. However, it had been a truly exciting day and this little glide had given us some great sport. Just to be able to find an unknown stretch of water like this and exploit it in these exceptional water conditions was reward enough.

By now it was mid afternoon; time was racing on and we still had more uncharted water to explore, so we made our way further upstream in the hope of finding more pockets of unexplored water. However, I couldn't help thinking as we walked up through the trees and I looked around at this wonderful stretch of water, that finding another such stretch was certainly going to be difficult.

A fine, fresh 6-lb salmon taken off the Banffshire Avon during a spell of high water.

CHAPTER 9

OCTOBER
AUTUMN IN THE BORDERS

October is an interesting and often bewildering month for the salmon-fisher, a time of transition. The days are growing shorter, yet daytime temperatures are often high with plenty of warm sunshine and water temperatures can fluctuate dramatically, particularly if night frosts occur; but with the autumn colours at their glorious best, what better time to be among the Border hills, on Tweed and its famous tributary, the Ettrick?

For many fishermen on Tweedside, autumn means fishing with slow- and fast-sink lines and 2–3-in brass tubes or Waddingtons; but this need not necessarily be the case. It is, as I have said, a time of transition, and one should be prepared to fish with a sinking line early in the day and to change up even to a floating line with a small summer fly during the warmer, middle part of the day.

My first day on Ettrick was a glorious bright, sunny morning and, though fairly breezy, pleasantly mild. Clearly it had not rained for some while, and the river was low and gin-clear. I had met the gillie at the estate office and I started at the top of the beat with the slow-sinking line and 2-in brass tube which he had recommended. I couldn't help feeling that the fly was far too heavy and large for such conditions, but I persisted for a while and then changed to similar tube, but without success.

My feeling was that the river needed more water – how many times do we say that during a fishing week? This was reinforced as the day became warm and I discarded jersey and jacket to fish in my shirt-sleeves. Lunchtime brought a lovely hatch of olives and I couldn't help feeling that a smaller fly must be a better bet.

After lunch I changed down to a 1-in aluminium tube, but despite this and various other changes of size and pattern, I remained blank for the day. Having seen only one salmon, I wasn't altogether surprised at my final tally!

Evening brought a change, with low cloud and persistent drizzle, but I remember thinking that more than a drizzle was needed to bring the river into spate. However, by next morning it had risen about a foot and was roaring down; plainly the hills upstream had seen some heavy rain overnight.

Luckily, the water hadn't coloured, and it looked perfect as the sky cleared to herald another bright, mild day. I felt sure the fresh water would bring a run of fish up from the lower Tweed beats, but though I fished every pool carefully with the big recommended tube, by lunchtime I hadn't felt so much as a tweak.

Back at the car I met the other two rods. One had caught a lovely fresh fish of about 6lb, a sink-tip line and a size 10 double Shrimp Fly having done the trick. Just to see a fish has an amazing effect on flagging spirits and it was with renewed confidence that I changed back to my black-and-yellow hairwing on a 1-in aluminium Aros tube.

By now the river was falling off, but it still looked in good ply. I fished carefully all afternoon, seeing just a couple of fresh fish running through, then, just before 5 pm, as the light was fading, the fly was coming into the side when I felt a good, solid pull and the reel screamed. Five minutes later I was able to beach my first fish, not a salmon but a lovely, shiny fresh sea-trout of a little more than 4lb. I was delighted, the small tube had indeed brought success.

The last hour into darkness often proves a great taking time, especially on Tweedside in the autumn. This is the time when the fresh-running fish seem to be settling into pools and taking up station in their lies. The changing light seems to make them more alert and keener to take.

Obligingly, the river rose again during the night and next morning was again in superb ply. Just before 11 am I was fishing through a pool called The Piggeries, which divides into Upper and Lower. Having fished through the Upper, I moved slowly through the neck of the Lower, which has a lovely deep tail – it looked a perfect lie. It was a difficult cast, with many overhanging branches and a large log wedged in the opposite bank, but my first effort was good and the little black-and-yellow tube dropped in under the overhang and swung slowly round to my side. It was literally dangling as I started a slow hand retrieve, and just as I did so, the line tightened, the rod bent and – BANG! – he was on! I played the fish for five or six minutes before I was able to beach him safely, another beautiful, shiny, fresh-run autumn salmon, weighing 7lb. It was a lovely, deep, short fish, and so fresh that I even looked for sea-lice on it. It had obviously run hard from the tidal water at Berwick.

I saw several other fish in the afternoon, no other offers were forthcoming; but I wasn't complaining! My fishing companion for the day had also taken a fine fresh fish in the afternoon at just over 16lb, again on a small fly. So, in two days one beat of this little spate river had produced three salmon and one sea-trout on small patterns that one would normally use in the summer.

That evening I bumped into Bill Currie in a restaurant in Melrose. 'Well, Neale, what are you doing tomorrow?' 'Going home, I think.' 'No, you're not! You're fishing my rod on Tweed!' How could I refuse?

I was on the beat bright and early next morning to find, to my surprise, that I had no 'opposition'. 'What luck', I thought. The weather was bright and sunny, but it had turned much colder overnight. The gauge showed the river at 1ft 1in – just right! I tackled up and decided to keep with my black-and-yellow Aros tube, but brass this time. I was going to fish the headstream of the large Birkie Pool, where the extra weight of the brass would be an advantage.

Wading in, I carefully put my Wet-Cel 2 across the fast stream, at the same time putting in a good upstream mend. I had been fishing for only a matter of minutes when the line whirred off the reel for several seconds. I let it go and lifted the rod, and then tightened just in time to feel the weight of the fish before he was away, I thought it was most probably a sea-trout. However, it was an exciting start to the day.

I moved slowly on down the pool and five minutes later pulled another fish. It was then that I decided to change to a black-and-orange tube of the same size. This fly had only just hit the water when it was grabbed, and again the reel screamed. After a none-too-spectacular fight I beached the fish to find it was a sea-trout kelt of 3–4lb, which was quickly returned to the water.

So far it had been an exciting morning, and it was still only 9.30 am. I carried on down the pool, and, as the fly swung round in deep water by some large rocks, known to be a good lie, the line slowly tightened and I lifted once again, to feel a good solid resistance before this fish, too, was gone. 'Damn! Should have let him have more time!' I thought. Then, downstream and close in to my bank, I saw a fish head-and-tail. I worked my way down slowly covering every inch of water, and at exactly the

Peter Heddle fishing the headstream of the Birkie Pool on Tweed in late October, with the autumn colours at their best.

129

spot I had seen the fish, the line tightened again. This time I let him have his head as line was taken off the reel. 'One . . . two . . . three . . . four . . .' I counted to myself, and then lifted the rod.

This time I'd made no mistake. He was mine! Or was he? He took off across the pool like a rocket before I could scramble out of the water and gain a foothold on the slippery bank! I was already down to my backing, but I managed to follow him down and soon regained line. Ten minutes later he was on his side and I was able to tail him out, a super fresh fish of 6lb.

It was only just after 10 am, and I had enjoyed more sport in an hour than in the previous three days! Once again, even with a drop in water temperature, the 1-in tube had proved its worth.

It was not to last. By lunchtime the day had changed, the mist had descended on the hills, a steady drizzle had begun to fall, and it was much cooler. I had no further offers for the rest of the day and saw hardly any fish, but I had seen some fast-and-furious sport in that earlier hour. Indeed, all four days had been most enjoyable, and more than enough incentive to tie-up a further selection of Aros tubes – small tubes!

CHAPTER 10

NOVEMBER
TWO DAYS ON TWEED

One of the wonderful things about being on Tweed at the back-end of the season, besides the autumn colours, is the opportunity to fish a first-class salmon river when virtually all other salmon fishing has come to a close. In Scotland, Nith and Tweed alone continue their seasons to the end of November, and those lucky enough to fish them can shorten their close season by an extra month.

It was in the first week of November that Annie had decided book herself into a rather posh health clinic, where she intended to do nothing but exercise, relax, and live on a diet of condensed carrot juice! Health clinics are not my idea of fun, so with salmon to be caught on Tweed, I phoned my good friend Charlie Miller, at the Tweed Valley Hotel in Walkerburn, to see if he had any fishing available. He was able to offer me just two days.

I had hoped to drive to Tweedside the evening before my first day, but I was delayed so I decided to have an early night and to get up at the crack of dawn and drive up so as to arrive on the river by mid-morning, all being well.

This was a mistake; basically because I was too excited to sleep properly, and when the alarm went off at 3 am I had snatched barely an hour of proper sleep. However, I soon had the car loaded and I was on the road north by 4 am, reporting to Charlie Miller by 10 am and feeling only slightly the worse for lack of sleep! By eleven o'clock I was on the river, having set up my double-handed Mackenzie Philps 15-footer with a slow-sinking line and one of my Aros specials dressed on a 1-in brass tube. Not much rain had fallen recently and my heart sank when I saw that the river was quite low. I doubted that I had much chance of sport, few fish had been taken during the week; but I had driven a long way and I was going to fish and enjoy my break come what may. It was a mild, dry and reasonably bright morning, and the autumn colours still lingered; I was happy just to be there.

Chatting briefly to Jim, the gillie, I was told me that some Norwegians were fishing further down and that I should try the top end of the beat. Another fishing tenant was about, but was not to be seen.

Wading across the river, I worked my way slowly down to one of my favourite pools. It takes a fast headstream and then slows as it turns gently into a long, slow bend. The pool is deep and often holds a good head of fish. It fishes well from my side, but trees make a double Spey-cast essential if the water is to be covered successfully.

Several fish were showing further down, and I felt optimistic as I started to work through the pool. However, once I passed the initial fast headstream, it became apparent that my little brass tube was slightly too heavy and was snagging on weeds and the bottom.

Deciding the depth at which to fish is often the difficulty when starting on any fishing trip. Should you use a sinking line and a lighter fly, or an intermediate line with a heavier fly? Is the fly too big or too small? These and other questions run through your mind, and until you feel that magical pull, persistent nagging doubts pervade your thoughts; and with only a couple of short November days available, the need to get things right is urgent. My decision this day was to stay with the slow-sinker and I opted for a lighter 1-in Waddington fairly sparsely dressed with a red-and-black hairwing. The water was also not only low, but gin-clear.

Fishing on down the pool, I had only the faintest pluck, which could well have been from a sea-trout. By now I could feel the lack of sleep and effects of the long drive catching up with me, so I opted to stop for some lunch. Soon I was joined by the other tenant, who seemed to view me suspiciously at first, believing me to be poaching from the beat below! I assured him that I was indeed a legitimate tenant and we sat and chatted. He'd taken a fine fish of 12lb earlier in the week further upstream, but alas nothing since.

After lunch we went our separate ways, myself to fish further up, and he to fish down through the bend; but by 3 pm I really had had enough, and decided that a couple of hours' sleep before dinner were indicated.

Going down to the bar at about 6 pm, I met some friends from a few years before. They confirmed that the fishing was difficult and that only two fish had been taken by all the rods! After dinner it was an early night for me, ready for an early start next morning.

I was on the river by just after 9 am, on another beautiful, mild autumn day. By mid-morning I was back on my favourite bend, with my small and lightly dressed Waddington, which seemed to be fishing well. Halfway down the pool, just where I was expecting it, I felt a good, solid pull followed by a quick scream from the reel – and then nothing! How can a fish with a fly in its mouth take off yards of line and drop it just like that? It has happened to me on several occasions, and now I always fish off the reel and let the fish take line. Normally, it will hook itself. It is an exciting way of fishing and usually effective! However, this fish was not to be, and despite covering the lie again, I could provoke no response.

My fellow-tenant joined me again and I learned that my 'event' was the only one of the day, but at least it gave some grounds for encouragement. Deciding to go back upstream to fish the pool where I had seen several fish moving earlier, I jokingly told him to keep his ears open in case I needed a hand with the net! This particular pool, The Mound, is normally fished from the other bank, but I thought a cast from my side might be worthwhile.

Extending a longish line, I was soon able to cover the whole pool, I was happy with both line and fly, which seemed to be fishing at just the right depth without

Bob Lambert fishing down to the mound on Holylee, River Tweed. This pool fishes well from both banks as Ian found out when chatting to the gillie.

catching the bottom. I was halfway down when Jim, the gillie, appeared on the other bank. 'Does this side fish as well as the other, Jim?' 'Oh, aye,' he said, and at that very second my line tightened and the reel screamed for several seconds. I lifted the rod to feel a good, solid resistance, and then a magnificent fresh fish leaped clear of the water and began a splendid account of itself, making my 15-footer work really hard.

Knowing that I had no place to beach the fish, Jim had managed to attract the attention of my friend downstream. Realising I was into a fish, he kindly came to help with the net, complaining light-heartedly about my interfering with his fishing time, and lifted a magnificent cock fish of 10½lb onto the bank for me. I think we were both equally delighted.

After a joint lunch and a few minutes to savour the atmosphere of Tweed at its finest, we split up once again and went

A great day to end the season with a genuine fresh-run salmon – Paul Huggett has every reason to look pleased with his first salmon of 10lb caught on Holylee, Tweed.

off in different directions. I decided to try upstream and to fish across and under a line of trees on the far bank where Jim had told me he had seen a large fish showing earlier. 'Just off the old fence post that drops into the water,' he said. 'That's where he is!' It is astonishing how many times a good lie seems to be 'just off the old fence'!

I walked slowly up in the bright, warm conditions. The pool had good depth under the far bank, but not too much speed in the current, so I decided on a lighter fly once again and to change to an intermediate line, size 11, which fishes nicely, just under the surface.

My chosen fly this time was a ¾-in aluminium tube, with a black-and-orange hairwing tied Tadpole-style, and trailing 2–3-in beyond the hook. It really does look good in the water. I extended line and after a minute or so was able to cast a long enough line to cover the far side just above the fence post. An underwater obstacle gave an extra run of stream here, and I lengthened line a little more on the next cast to put the fly into the streamy stretch. The cast was perfect and as the fly hit the water, so it was seized in a most savage take. Line screamed off the reel and I let the fish have its way as it tore downstream. By the time I lifted and tightened, I was already on to my backing!

'This is incredible,' I thought, and decided it was time to slow him down. As I applied pressure I saw him jump clear of the water and thought that, despite all the fuss, it wasn't such a large fish after all; but he continued to put up a good fight and I knew he must be well hooked. Several minutes later I had him on his side and then safely up the beach. It was only then that I realised what I had captured – not a salmon, but one of Tweed's marvellous late running sea-trout, reasonably fresh and weighing just over 6½lb. It had been one of those memorable takes of which one dreams – and what a superb finish to my two days!

The first week of November had been brilliant: 1ft 4in on the gauge at Scrogbank and six salmon with a best fish of 21lb in five days' of fishing, who could have wished for better? As I returned south it poured and poured, nearly two weeks of solid rain and Tweed went into a massive, coloured flood! The rain eased and the weather was incredibly mild, almost tropical in fact, as Michael and I made our way northwards from Sheffield for the last three days of the season.

We were like a couple of giggling schoolboys as we stopped on the bridge at Ashiestiel and peered into the gin-clear water of Tweed below. The gauge now measured 1ft 6in and conditions had never been better for fifteen years; 'a great chance of a fish', said the recording we listened to on Tweedline and we couldn't believe our luck.

We were fishing on the top beat for the morning and changing over at lunchtime. 'Tiger country, I call it up there,' said Tony the gillie, 'well worth the effort, but watch out for the wading in Nowt Sykes, it's a little up and down!' That was the understatement of the year. I started in at Stiel Pool wading carefully down the edge; it wasn't long before I saw a fish show on the far side and then another below it. 'Running fish,' I thought, however, the signs looked promising. It was so mild and the water temperature was a high 46°F, quite remarkable for the end of November. I was fishing my Daiwa Amorphous 15ft 6in rod with a Wet-Cel 2 and a small black-and-orange Waddington which had been so successful for me just three weeks earlier.

I'd been fishing for about thirty minutes, and suddenly I felt the line tighten and a fast scream off the reel. It turned out to be a sea-trout kelt of about 3lb which was carefully unhooked and quickly returned to the water. By late autumn the sea-trout have usually spawned and can be easily identified by a long and thin shape and swollen vent. They often retain a silvery sheen and can still give a good account of themselves. It is sad how many of these fish are killed in ignorance, being mistaken for fresh fish, usually ending up lying on display in the hotel reception like a well worn wallet!

The morning passed quickly and we saw good numbers of fresh fish running hard. The rods fishing below us had taken a fresh fish off the middle beat, which lifted our hopes for the afternoon. It was a glorious sunny afternoon and very warm. Gladdies Weil was just full of fish, many of them stale residents just crashing around in their usual lies, but many fresh fish were coming through with their heads down and running for the upper spawning grounds at a rate of knots. We fished hard until the light faded at about 4.30 pm but without so much as an offer. We were awake early the next morning and from our B & B high up at 1,200 feet we could see that it was a beautiful sunny morning, still with evidence of a hard frost shining off the car. As we descended into the Tweed Valley an icy-cold mist was still keeping a hold over the river and our rod rings were freezing hard. This cold mist refused to burn off until after lunch and the morning only produced one tentative offer to a black-and-orange Aros tube. We were keen to get down to the lower beat as the conditions began to improve, and at this time of year the afternoons are extremely short. Our friends fishing below us had scored yet again, taking a fish apiece in the morning, and we were already halfway through our trip. I was beginning to wonder what we were doing wrong! We seemed to be always in the wrong place at the wrong time, or was it the right place at the wrong time?

A beautiful day on the Tweed with falling water and 'expectations' of a fresh fish for Max Fraser.

Michael was keen to fish the House Pool while I went to the top pool called the Electric. I fished through the delightful Electric and carried on down through to the Boat Pool. Suddenly, the river had gone dead and there was not not a sign of a fish showing anywhere. Michael had taken a sea-trout of about 4lb in the House Pool, which took the fly as he was hand-lining back and was duly returned to the water. He then went in above me and pulled another fish on a yellow Ally's Shrimp in the Electric; it was obviously his day. Again our short afternoon began to close in as the cold mist descended upon us sending the air temperature plummeting quickly. The river had gone quite dead and our expectations of Sunday were beginning to subside. However, we still had one day left.

St Andrew's Day dawned clear and bright, with a carpet of frost on the ground. As we made our way down to the lower beat, conditions for our last day looked better. Michael and I both made our way to the top of the beat to fish Electric and Boat. The water level had dropped off by several inches now, owing to the heavy overnight frosts and, therefore, the House Pool was becoming rather too slow for the fly.

Tony, the gillie, took me into the Boat Pool to start, but despite seeing several good fish, my black-and-orange Waddington was totally ignored. Michael had gone further up into the Electric, fishing his favoured yellow Ally's Shrimp. Yet again he had seen fish running through and had managed to pull another fish! I came back and followed him down through this pool. He spotted a fish towards the tail of the pool and covered it. The fly was taken first time and before I knew it Michael was on the bank, rod bent double, as the fish was now running hard and fast back into the Boat Pool. By the time I caught up with him, he was well down in the Boat Pool and the fish was ready for the net, a fine hen fish of around 12lb which was quickly unhooked and released; his first Tweed salmon! After lunch we moved back onto the top beat, it was a glorious mild autumn day and conditions were excellent. Michael and I fished the Rookery, but saw nothing; the Stiel was also quiet. We figured that our best bet was going to be Nowt Sykes right in the heart of 'Tiger Country'! It really is a superb pool with a fast headstream right through to the middle, which gradually turns out into a slower pace over some huge boulders offering excellent lies for the fish. However, the steep, wooded bank on our side means that it can only be waded, and I have to say it is a nightmare, as the rocky terrain makes for some hair-raising wading to say the least!

By 3.30 pm the light was beginning to fade, the wind had eased and the pool looked ideal. Several fish started to show and it appeared another run of fish were coming through. Michael was following me down, and I had changed onto my old favourite black-and-orange Aros on a 1-in brass tube to try and cover these deeper streamy holes. I had already snagged on one or two weedy outcrops from these rocks, but by and large I felt confident with the way the fly was fishing. Then it happened, just as the fly swung across the fast middle stream it just stopped in mid-water. At first I lifted carefully, but nothing happened. I moved the rod tip up, and it appeared to be snagged on one of these rocks. I lifted a little harder thinking two good thumps should shift it, when, suddenly the fish took off like a rocket across the pool and turned a spectacular cartwheel. It was a big fresh fish, and I managed to keep control as it ran back towards me, when suddenly, before I knew what had happened, the hooks were out and my St Andrew's Day trophy was gone. Michael, still fishing above me, hand on hip, stared in disbelief; he fished on through the gloaming without saying a word. Before we knew it our season was suddenly over. It could have been a spectacular finish, but it was not to be. We had enjoyed ourselves, as always, but now it was time to celebrate the closing with just a small measure, or two, and thoughts of another season to come, not too far away now!

In conditions of high falling water, fish will lie close to the bank. The careful angler should not wade, but fish a short, controlled line to search out every possible lie.

For holiday anglers the 1991 season was without doubt a season to be forgotten, both for the lack of rain during the summer and the scarcity of grilse and back-end salmon. On upper Tweed, where I usually fish in the back-end, it was all too apparent that, despite excellent water levels from early November, and a good stock of fish in the lower river, fish weren't in the upper river in any quantity, with hardly a sighting of those big, cock 'kippers' that we normally see.

Early November had seen me fishing with my old friend Bill Currie on our little upper Tweed beat, and he was kind enough to ask me back for the last two days of the season in the hope that an eleventh-hour run of fish would appear. Annie and I left Suffolk in mid-afternoon and arrived in the Borders after a comfortable six-hour drive to be greeted with lashings of rain. Having prayed for rain all summer, I now found myself quietly saying, 'Please, God, no more! That will do nicely, thank you!'

Next morning I was up at crack of dawn and poked my head out of the door. My prayers had been answered. In the dawn light the air was cool and I could see the river running clear and steady. 'Wonderful!' I thought.

The back-end days of November are short, and I was keen to get on the water early to make the most of my precious two days. By 8.30 am I was tackled-up and ready to go, but to my surprise other rods were already out, including the opposition. I couldn't believe it! It was a mild, misty morning, with more than a hint

The closing days of November are short and the light often fades by 4 pm: that last hour can be a magical time to be fishing for salmon

of rain in the air again, but a glance at the gauge confirmed excellent water conditions, the river holding at 1ft 6in and running gin-clear.

Finding the right recipe for success in two short autumn days is often difficult. With summer fishing the choice is fairly easy: floating lines and smallish flies; autumn and spring fishing demands a consideration of water height, temperature and colour. Some people maintain that the use of sinking lines makes it a matter of 'chuck-and-chance-it', which to some degree, may be true; but when a fish takes, and if you are fishing off the reel, as I do, what a wonderful feeling that initial contact gives as the line tightens and the reel emits that wonderful scream. It makes my heart thump!

I cast my eye over my boxes of Waddingtons and Aros tubes and wondered which one it was to be. Line size was no problem, I usually fish in autumn and early spring with a #11 Wet-Cel 2, which seems perfect for my type of fishing and, by and large, sinks at an ideal rate without raking the bottom at every other cast. After careful scrutiny, I decided to opt for a 2-in black-and-orange Waddington. Even so, as I waded down the fast headstream of the Birkie Pool, and the Waddington swam in to the bank, I couldn't help feeling that I was fishing too light. I persisted, and as I progressed into the slower and deeper water, I felt happier that the fly was now at the correct depth and fishing properly. This pool is a long one and can hold fish over its entire length, though most tend to lie on our side, especially at this height of water. Today, however, after three hours of careful searching, I had spotted only one fish, which for the time of year, was ridiculous.

Taking an early lunch, I decided to go further upstream and try Scrogbank Burn pool. My companion, Ian Calcott, was going to keep trying Birkie; he thought a small run of fish had come into the pool just before lunch, and that had lifted his hopes!

At Scrogbank I waded carefully in at the burn and put out a shortish line. Salmon often lie just off the burn mouth, and it is important not to wade in too far or cast too long. After a couple of casts, line whirred off the reel. I let it run for what seemed like minutes, then lifted the rod and set the hooks. I knew at once that it wasn't a salmon, and, sure enough, after several minutes, I had the fish beaten and on its side – a well-mended hen sea-trout kelt of about 4lb.

A surprising number of sea-trout kelts are caught in October and November and are unfortunately mistaken by anglers for clean fish. Sea-trout usually spawn much earlier than salmon, and anglers should always be aware of that fact and be on the look-out for those tell-tale signs of a kelt. Sea-trout certainly retain a shininess, which makes them look in good condition, but they are also long and thin, with extended vents and flat, or slightly inverted stomachs. Such fish must always be carefully returned. I managed to keep the fish in shallow water while I quickly dislodged the hooks, and she shot off into deep water. I fished right through the pool, but saw not another fish move, which was most unusual.

The short November day soon closed in. The hills became mistier and the chill of evening had crept into the air by 3.30 pm. I'd also had a nasty leaking left wader boot, and my foot was gradually going numb! I decided to take an early bath, but to visit Ted Hunter at Angler's Choice in Melrose on the way. In times of emergency like this he willingly makes urgent repairs and steam-welds patches on to boots in a most professional manner. 'Be ready by 8 am, Sir,' he said – and so they were! With that call to make I was up even earlier next morning, only to find that now one of my car tyres had a puncture! This wouldn't have inspired confidence at any time, but on the last day of the season . . .

After all that, and with Annie urging me on, I still managed to be on my beat by 9 am. Not bad going! When Annie wants to get me onto the water, she doesn't hang about!

The mist had cleared and the day soon became bright and mild; it felt altogether a much better fishing day than the previous one, and the gauge confirmed that the river had dropped by a couple of inches. 'Excellent!' I thought.

Starting at the head of the Birkie again, I elected to try one of my old favourite flies – a black-and-yellow Aros hairwing dressed on a 1-in tube. At this height of water it would fish well in the fast headstream and wouldn't snag on the bottom in the slower water. It fished perfectly, and I really felt I had the recipe right. Several fish moved as I worked my way down, but none seemed to be in a taking mood. Then, suddenly, I heard a fish jump and a reel screamed behind me on the opposite bank! The opposition had cracked it and landed a fine 13-pounder after a considerable fight.

Hiding my true feelings, I called across, 'Well done, lovely fish!', took a big gulp, counted to ten, and quietly went about my business once again, feeling frustrated but also slightly more optimistic. However, at lunchtime I was still blank, with only hours of the season remaining. Bill, too, had been unable to connect.

Back at the top pool after lunch, the water looked perfect. Halfway down, in midstream, my fly was pulled hard, the reel screamed briefly, and the fish was gone. It wasn't a big fish, and probably a sea-trout, but the adrenalin flowed and my enthusiasm renewed; but success was elusive, and I decided to walk down to rejoin Bill who by now was well down towards the tail of the Long Birkie Pool.

The change of scene renewed my optimism, and with the change of light on such a fine day, the chance of a fish would now be better. Changing to a 1-in black-and-orange tube, I let Annie give it her female blessing. 'It's those female pheromones,' she said, 'they'll do the trick!'

I was somewhat sceptical, but after what followed, I am now a full-blooded pheromone convert!

It was just after 3 pm, and I was only too aware that I had only and hour or so of daylight left – only an hour or so of the season – and then it would all be over until next year.

I fished on for forty-five minutes and with the light really fading I was not far behind the opposition, who seemed to be moving infuriatingly slowly! I had seen several fish rolling and was feeling quite optimistic. I could just make out the *plop* as the little tube entered the water . . .

The fly swung slowly back in to my side and I had just started to retrieve line when suddenly the line stopped and tightened. I lifted, felt the fish and carefully climbed onto the bank. It felt a hefty fish and made two solid runs off the reel before the hooks came out! I couldn't believe it. How could this happen on the last day of the season? It was most unfair! 'Come on, Neale! You've still got ten minutes left, and it's a long close season!' a voice inside my head commanded.

Carefully I dropped into the water again, pulled off line and began to cast. Just then Bill appeared in the half-light and I told him of my bad luck. A fish splashed above me. 'What am I doing talking?' said Bill, and he waded in some 20yd above me.

A couple of casts later, and couple of paces downstream, the action started again, but this time the fish really took hold and tore line off the reel. I let him have his head before I lifted and tightened. 'That's more like it, Ian!' called Bill, while I heard the opposition below me mutter, 'That's made me really sick!' I was feeling absolutely delighted!

The fish was a real acrobat and cleared the water several times. At first I thought it might be a sea-trout, but after a tremendous fight lasting several minutes I had it on its side and in the shallows and Bill was able to net it safely in virtual darkness – a cracking and quite fresh fish of 7lb. We were both jubilant. What a way to end the day!

As we walked back to the hut, a brace of duck flighted upstream, a bat circled overhead, and a lone woodcock flew out of the trees and over Tweed. In the near darkness, we heard a fish roll. What a way to end the season!

As the light fades and another season draws to a close, 30 November on Tweed, two anglers make their way down Birkie Pool for the 'last chance'.

INDEX